100 DEADLIEST THINGS ON THE PLANET

Conceived, edited, and designed by Marshall Editions
The Old Brewery
6 Blundell Street
London N7 9BH

ISBN 978-0-545-43437-9

Publisher: James Ashton-Tyler
Editorial director: Sorrel Wood
Editorial project manager: Emily Collins
Designer: Tina Vaughan
Production: Nikki Ingram

Printed and bound in China by Toppan Leefung Printing Ltd.

10 9 8 7 6 5 4 3 2 1   12 13 14 15 16

First printing, September 2012

Anna Claybourne

100
DEADLIEST
THINGS ON
THE PLANET

CONTENTS

Introduction 6

Animals that Attack . . . 8

Tiger 9
Lion. 10
Jaguar. 11
Leopard 12
Cougar. 13
Elephant 14
Rhino. 15
Wolf 16
Wolverine 17
Wild boar. 18
African buffalo 19
Brown bear 20
Polar bear 21
Hippo 22
Leopard seal 23
Cassowary. 24
Pitohui. 25
Ostrich 26
Eagle. 27

Killer Reptiles and Fierce Fish 28

Komodo dragon 29
Crocodile 30
American alligator. 31
Poison dart frog 32
Bushmaster 33
Inland taipan. 34
Indian cobra 35
Reticulated python 36
Boomslang. 37
Mamba 38
Russell's viper 39
Australian brown snake 40
Death adder. 41
Beaked sea snake 42
Electric eel. 43
Tiger shark. 44
Great white shark 45
Bull shark. 46
Goliath tiger fish. 47
Stonefish 48
Puffer fish 49
Needlefish 50
Stingray. 51

Bloodthirsty Beasties 52
Blue-ringed octopus 53
Box jellyfish 54
Portuguese man-of-war 55
Cone shell 56
Flatworm 57
Mosquito 58
Tsetse fly 59
Locust 60
Asian giant hornet 61
Killer bee 62
Tick 63
Deathstalker scorpion 64
Fat-tailed scorpion 65
African safari ant 66
Fire ant 67
Kissing bug 68
Black widow spider 69
Brazilian wandering spider 70
Funnel-web spider 71

Disasters, Poisons, and Deadly Diseases 72
False morel 73
Destroying angel 74
Poison parsnip 75
Deadly nightshade 76
Castor bean plant 77
Strychnine tree 78
Foxglove 79
Wolfsbane 80

Food poisoning 81
Botulism 82
Radiation poisoning 83
Rabies 84
Tetanus 85
Japanese encephalitis 86
Ebola 87
Smallpox 88
Black Death 89
Cholera 90
Leprosy 91
Earthquake 92
Sinkhole 93
Volcanic eruption 94
Landslide 95
Avalanche 96
Quicksand 97
Drought 98
Heat wave 99
Wildfire 100
Sandstorm 101
Tornado 102
Tropical cyclone 103
Ice storm 104
Tsunami 105
Iceberg 106
Riptide 107
Limnic eruption 108
Whirlpool 109
Solar flare 110
Impact event 111

Acknowledgments 112

INTRODUCTION

It's a dangerous world out there. You might feel safe . . . but don't get too comfortable! You don't have to go far to find the killer creatures or lethal germs featured in this book. They're everywhere!

BE AFRAID, VERY AFRAID

Man-eating monsters, poisonous plants, vicious viruses, and wild weather . . . all of these things can be killers. Some of them, like mosquitoes and droughts, have been responsible for millions upon millions of deaths throughout human history. Others, like tigers or quicksand, might be less likely to harm you—but if you did have a close encounter with them, it could be seriously bad news.

DO YOU KNOW . . .

- What's more deadly— sharks or bees?
- Why a kiss from a kissing bug could kill?
- How to tell if you've caught the Black Death?
  Read on to find out!

STUCK AT HOME?

OK, don't panic. Many of the deadly horrors you will meet in this book are quite rare, like smallpox, sinkholes, or Komodo dragons. For the rest, there are modern medicines, safety precautions, and plain old common sense. You wouldn't poke a deadly snake, annoy an ostrich, go swimming in a whirlpool, or eat a mysterious mushroom you found in the woods, would you? Let's hope not!

DON'T POKE A SLEEPING BEAR

It goes without saying that deadly things can be pretty hazardous to your health. This book does give you a few tips on how to avoid them, or how to deal with them if you have to. But if you ever are in a real-life deadly situation, it's important to stay calm, keep your wits about you, and follow the instructions you are given. And **DON'T** go looking for deadly things on purpose!

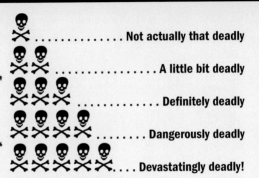

DEADLY DEGREE

☠ . . . . Not actually that deadly

☠☠ . . . . A little bit deadly

☠☠☠ . . . . Definitely deadly

☠☠☠☠ . . . . Dangerously deadly

☠☠☠☠☠ . . . . Devastatingly deadly!

ANIMALS THAT ATTACK

There are some killer creatures that would have us for lunch without batting an eyelid. You probably know that tigers, lions, and bears are not to be messed with. But did you know that some of the deadliest creatures on the planet are seemingly peaceful plant eaters, like elephants and hippos? And birds can be killers, too—even small ones that could sit in your hand.

TIGER

Imagine a pet cat grabbing and devouring a tiny mouse. A tiger can do the same thing to a wild boar, a large deer—or even a human!

DEADLY BITE

A tiger usually catches its prey by sneaking up behind it silently. It gets closer and closer, until it's within pouncing range. Then it leaps, aiming to grab its victim's back or neck. The tiger drags the victim to the ground and bites its throat to kill it. The tiger's huge, strong jaws can bite down so hard, they can crunch right through skulls and backbones—ouch!

A TASTE FOR HUMANS

Most tigers eat deer and other animals, not people. But in some places, especially parts of India, they do hunt humans. If tigers live close to villages or fishing areas, they may begin to see people as prey, especially if they're hungry.

A tiger's sharp teeth are perfect for grabbing and killing prey.

DEADLY DEGREE

☠ ☠ ☠

Attacks are rare—but if a tiger wants to eat you, it will!

LION

Lions have killed hundreds of people, and made a meal of many of them. But we're small and bony compared to a lion's favorite foods, like zebra and wildebeest. So why eat us?

DON'T WAKE THE LION!

Lions love to lie around snoozing, and hate being disturbed. That makes for an angry lion. So does approaching a lion busy enjoying its hard-earned meal of fresh meat—it will attack you if it thinks you want to steal its dinner!

SICK BUT STILL DEADLY

Lions sometimes switch to a diet of humans if they're ill or wounded. People can't run very fast, so we make an easy target for a hungry lion that's too sick to chase an antelope or zebra. Lions may hunt us if they run out of their normal food. Their prey can sometimes run short due to diseases or if humans hunt and kill them.

A lion devours his prey in the Masai Mara reserve in Kenya.

DEADLY DEGRE

☠ ☠ ☠

Lions are hungry for fresh meat, don't care where it comes fror

DR. LIVINGSTONE, I PRESUME? RRAARRGH!

A lion tried to eat the famous Victorian explorer David Livingstone in Africa in the 1840s. He described his narrow escape: "The lion caught me by the shoulder and we both came to the ground together. Growling horribly, he shook me as a terrier dog does a rat." Livingstone survived, but his arm never worked properly again.

JAGUAR

The majestic, muscle-bound black-spotted jaguar lives in South America, where it's the biggest cat in the wild. Its jaws can crunch through the skull of a large deer or wild boar—and could do the same to us.

ANGRY ATTACKS

Jaguars are famous for their wild, bad-tempered ways—and when they attack, they are seriously deadly. They are extra-dangerous when guarding their cubs, or when kept in zoos. Jaguars are hard to tame, unpredictable, and unfriendly—probably because they would rather be hiding in the forest! Zookeepers have to take care, as jaguars have been known to kill them.

Beware this snarling jaguar. He is deadly quiet and black as the night.

SCARY NAME

The jaguar's name comes from a local Native American word, *yaguara*—"the beast that kills in a single bound."

SPOT THE JAGUAR

If you go to the South American rain forest, you might see jaguar footprints—but it's hard to see an actual jaguar. They live deep in the jungle and avoid humans. This might be because they have traditionally been hunted for their skins, so they have learned to avoid us at all costs.

BEWARE OF THE BEAST!

Rain forest peoples are very scared of jaguars, even though attacks are rare. These fears probably date from long ago, when humans didn't have guns. This meant jaguars were less afraid of us, and ate more people!

DEADLY DEGREE

One of the most lethal wild animals, if it wants to be!

LEOPARD

People don't usually think of leopards as scary people-eaters. They probably haven't heard of the deadly killer leopards of Rudraprayag and Panar. . . .

DEADLY DEGREE

☠ ☠ ☠

Surprisingly deadly,
for its small size.

A wandering leopard takes his victim by surprise in India—scary!

LEOPARDS ON THE LOOSE

Leopards belong to the "big cat" family, but they're only about half the size of a lion or tiger. However, they can still be very dangerous, especially in India. India has a huge population, with many people living in the countryside. Wild leopards wander into villages—sometimes even houses—and will attack if they are cornered.

KILLER CREATURES

A leopard can get a taste for human flesh, especially if it can't catch other prey. Two famous leopards went on deadly rampages in India, around 100 years ago. The leopard of Rudraprayag killed 125 people, and the even deadlier leopard of Panar gobbled up 400!

LOOK UP! Of all big cats, leopards are the best climbers. A leopard will often wait in a tree until something tasty wanders along, then drop down onto it for the kill. Be careful when going for a walk!

COUGAR

The cougar is a big, fierce wild cat found in mountains, deserts, and forests in North and South America. Like a kangaroo or a flea, it has extra-large back legs that help it to make huge, bounding leaps.

UNEXPECTED AMBUSH

Cougars are skilled at sneaking up and ambushing deer, goats, and hares. They hide in bushes or on a rocky ledge, then pounce onto their prey in a surprise attack. They pin it down with their paws, and give it a killer bite on the neck, throat, or head.

Cougars are so fierce they are sometimes called mountain lions.

DO COUGARS EAT PEOPLE?

Yes, starving cougars have been known to attack humans for food. Often, people manage to fight cougars off, or scare them away by screaming. But cougar attacks can be deadly, and several people are killed each year. Cougars don't often attack a group of people. They jump out on lone hikers, or children who are running around away from their group. Cougar attacks have become more common since the 1980s, mainly because more people are living, hiking, and camping in cougar country. An 11-year-old boy in Canada was nearly ambushed by a cougar, but his golden-retriever dog jumped in the way, saving the boy's life! Luckily, the pet dog survived, too!

BOIIING!

A cougar can bound so far and so high, it could jump right over a bus, from the front to the back. If one jumped on you, you wouldn't see it coming!

DEADLY DEGREE

Cougars can be killers, but most attack victims survive.

ELEPHANT

The slowly strolling, plant-eating elephant is often seen as a calm, intelligent creature. Yet elephants kill hundreds of people each year. When they turn nasty, it's time to run!

Even an enraged baby elephant can trample a truck!

MOTHERS ON THE RAMPAGE

Whatever you do, don't annoy an elephant, or get too close to one that's in a bad mood. If a mother elephant thinks another animal, or a human, is threatening her calf, she will charge, thundering toward her target at up to 25 mph (40 km/h). Elephants kill their enemies by trampling on them, or stabbing them with their long tusks. Once an elephant starts to charge, it's pretty bad news.

MAD MALES IN MUSTH

Every year, for a month, older male elephants become aggressive as they prepare to mate. An elephant in this state, called musth, might go on the rampage through a village. A zoo elephant may even suddenly turn against its keeper.

DEADLY DEGREE

Unpredictable and bad-tempered makes for a deadly mixture!

TERRIFYING TUSKS

An elephant's tusks are two of its front teeth that grow to an enormous length. They can be more than 7 feet (2 m) long— longer than a man is tall!

RHINO

Rhinos are the third-largest land animals after hippos and elephants. And, like their giant plant-eating cousins, they have a habit of going on a deadly rhino rampage!

HUNTERS

Rhinos have a reason to be suspicious of humans. Some people hunt them for their horns, which are made into medicines. People kill many more rhinos than rhinos kill people.

CHAAAAAARGE!

Not only are rhinos big and heavy, with massive horns on their noses, they are also fast. A black rhino gallops like a horse, at 40 mph (60 km/h)—much faster than elephants. Luckily, many charges are "bluffs." The rhino runs toward you but then stops and wanders off. But when a rhino is charging, you can't tell whether this will happen! The only way to be safe is not to bother rhinos at all.

I'd move out of the path of this charging rhino, if I were you!

DEADLY DEGREE

☠ ☠

Capable of trampling almost anything in its way.

WOLF

In fairy tales and movies, wolves are big and scary, with their horrible howling, slavering jaws, and deadly taste for human flesh. But are they really like that?

BEWARE OF THE WOLF!
Hundreds of years ago, wolves really were dangerous killers. They were more common than they are today—they lived all over the United States, Canada, Europe, and most of Asia. If you went on a journey in the countryside, you had to watch out for wolves! They hunted in packs, and could easily surround and drag down an adult human.

A wolf with a bloody face guards its kill from other hungry mouths.

DEADLY DEGREE

Hairy, scary, and fierce, but rarely deadly these days.

WILD WOLVES
Today, you're less likely to meet a hungry wolf, as they live mainly in the wilderness, far away from people. They are also shy and usually avoid us. But, once in a while, wolves still jump out on hikers or joggers, and in India they sometimes snatch children from forest villages. Usually, wolves that attack us are desperate for food, or are "rabid"—meaning they have the disease rabies (see page 84).

DID YOU KNOW?
Pet dogs actually attack and kill more people than wild wolves. Most wolves are peaceful, but some can be deadly if they decide to bite.

WOLVERINE

Would you want to mess with an animal nicknamed the "demon of the North," or "Indian devil"? Wolverines are quite small—but they are among the most ferocious creatures on the planet.

KILLING POWER

When a wolverine attacks, it jumps on its prey and uses its razor-sharp teeth and claws to tear it apart. Wolverines are tough, superstrong, and incredibly brave—they rarely give up in a fight. They weigh only about 33 pounds (15 kg), as much as a small dog. Yet, a single wolverine has been known to bring down a 330-pound (150-kg) reindeer! That's like you taking on a large tiger, on your own, and killing it.

Wolverines' big feet help them walk on snow.

I'LL HAVE THAT!

Wolverines will also fight other large animals, such as bears, to try to scare them off and steal their food. They have no fear! They definitely could be dangerous to us, too—but, luckily, they are very shy around humans. A wolverine would attack you only if you hurt, trapped, or cornered it.

DEADLY DEGREE

It definitely could kill and eat you—but rarely attacks humans.

X-MENTION

The *X-Men* character Wolverine is a superhero with powerful, fanglike teeth, and giant retractable claws on each hand.

WILD BOAR

The plump, pink pigs you see on farms were bred from a very different-looking animal—the hairy, razor-tusked wild boar. It's fierce, up to 6.5 feet (2 m) long, and sometimes deadly.

PIGGY PROBLEM

Can pigs really be deadly, marauding, wild beasts? Yes, they can! Problems for people usually arise when they disturb wild boars or try to hunt them. Boars are brave fighters and will battle to defend themselves, biting their attacker with big, sharp tusks.

This wild boar is giving a great view of his killer tusks.

PECCARY PACKS

In Central and South America, there are wild pigs called peccaries. They travel in herds, and if they feel threatened, they chatter their teeth loudly, then attack with their fanglike tusks. A pack of peccaries can even kill a jaguar (see page 11), and could effortlessly kill a human, though luckily, this is very rare.

DEADLY DEGREE

☠

You're very unlikely to die even in a ferocious wild boar attack.

DINO-PIG

Wild boars' prehistoric cousin, Dinohyus, was as big as a rhinoceros and far deadlier than a wild boar.

AFRICAN BUFFALO

African buffalo are like big, bulky, black cows, with long, floppy ears and handlebar-shaped horns. Like any cow, they wander to and fro, munching on grass. So what's so deadly about a herd of cows?

GORY GORING

Buffalo are dangerous in the same way as an angry bull—they use their horns to gore, or stab, their enemies. They also have sharp hooves and can trample you to death. Their horns are very wide and pointed, and can inflict horrific injuries. With one swipe of its head, a buffalo can tear its enemy wide open.

A NASTY END

In Africa, around 200 people a year die from buffalo attacks. Buffalo can kill other animals, such as lions. In fact, they're so dangerous, they are given the nickname "Black Death."

I'LL GET YOU BACK!

Big game hunters used to say buffalo that were shot and wounded would try to get revenge. They would sneak around in a circle, hide in the bushes, then charge at the hunter by surprise!

Charge! A buffalo on the rampage could make the ground shake!

BULKY BUFFALO

A big male buffalo can weigh up to 2,200 pounds (1,000 kg)—that's as heavy as some cars. You wouldn't have much chance with that standing on top of you!

DEADLY DEGREE

☠ ☠ ☠

Pretty deadly, for a cow!

BROWN BEAR

The idea of being eaten by a bear terrifies most people. Some bears are so strong, they can kill a human with one bite, or one swipe of a superpowerful paw.

You wouldn't want to be caught in these choppers.

SCARED OF THE BEAR

Brown bears vary in type, from Syrian bears the size of dogs, to grizzly bears, to Kodiak bears that can be up to 10 feet (3 m) tall. They have massive jaws, sharp claws up to 4 inches (10 cm) long, and incredible strength. Not surprisingly, people worry about bear attacks when they go hiking, camping, or fishing in bear country. If you do meet a bear, you can usually scare it away by waving or shouting.

WHEN BEARS ATTACK

Bears can be very deadly if they have cubs or food they want to protect. And, if a bear gets into the habit of stealing from trash cans or campsites, it may attack anyone in its way. Angry bears attack by biting and clawing.

STAY SAFE IN BEAR COUNTRY

• Hike in a group and stick to paths—don't wander in the wilderness!
• Make noise—bears will avoid you.
• Keep garbage wrapped up, and store it away from your tent.

DEADLY DEGREE

☠ ☠ ☠ ☠
✕ ✕ ✕ ✕

Most bears don't attack, but th are extremely deadly if they do

POLAR BEAR

Polar bears have a cute, cuddly image. You see them in wildlife documentaries about caring mothers and playful cubs—or as snuggly toys. So it's easy to forget just how deadly they are.

BEAR SCARES

A polar bear is a massive, strong, killer carnivore. Polar bears live in and around the Arctic. They mainly eat seals, but when they come across humans, they have been known to try to get into cars, and to attack people who tried to photograph them. They are so strong that they can kill people easily—a terrifying thought!

POLAR BEARS IN TOWN

Every fall, the town of Churchill, in northern Canada, fills up with polar bears on their way to hunt seals. The bears are a tourist attraction and are carefully protected, but they can also be a problem. They raid stores and have even attacked townspeople.

A fierce, hungry polar bear hunts in Norway.

SCARY BEAR STATS

Polar bears really are BIG. A male can be 10 feet (3 m) long, 6.5 feet (2 m) high, and can weigh up to 1,750 pounds (800 kg)—as much as 10 men!

DEADLY DEGREE

An incredibly bloodthirsty Arctic animal.

HIPPO

When you think of a hippo, you think of a fat, slow, peaceful creature, lazing in a muddy river. But in Africa, where they live, people are terrified of hippos. Why is that?

HIPPO HORROR

Hippos are massive, and can run fast. They can be 16 feet (5 m) long and weigh 6,600 pounds (3,000 kg)—the size of a pickup truck! If you annoy them, they can charge at you and crush you flat. They also have giant front teeth, up to 20 inches (50 cm) long—the length of a man's arm! Though they eat only plants, an angry hippo can bite a person, or even a boat, in two! In fact, they are thought to kill more people than any other large wild animal.

WHAT MAKES A HIPPO MAD?

Hippos are irritable. They don't like anyone going near their calves, or in their area of river.

When on land, they hate anything getting in between them and the water. In fact, they can't stand being bothered by anyone, anytime! Any of these things can lead to a horrific hippo attack.

DEADLY DEGREE

The hippo gets five for its lethal combination of killer qualities.

Stay clear of this hungry hippo's enormous jaws.

FIGHT TO THE DEATH

Male hippos fight for the position of group leader. They slash at one another with their long teeth, and sometimes the loser bleeds to death.

LEOPARD SEAL

The leopard seal is actually like an underwater leopard—it's as fierce as any big cat. It zooms through the icy seas around Antarctica, terrorizing and snapping up other sea creatures.

MIGHTY MOUTH

The leopard seal grows to almost 13 feet (4 m) long—the length of a car. It has a huge, powerful head, with immense jaws that can open incredibly wide. It uses them to grab whole penguins, large fish, and even other seals. There's no doubt this seal could gobble us up, too. But would it?

SEAL STORIES

Leopard seal attacks on humans have happened only a handful of times. In 1915, a leopard seal chased an Antarctic explorer, slithering after him over the ice. And, in 2003, a scientist died after a leopard seal bit her while she was snorkeling. These leopard seals may have mistaken people for seals or penguins—they normally don't see humans as food!

A vicious leopard seal races after its prey—teeth first!

PENGUIN GIFTS

One photographer went diving to take pictures of an enormous female leopard seal. The seal kept catching penguins and bringing them to him as little gifts.

DEADLY DEGREE

☠ ☠

Fast and fearsome, but luckily far away!

CASSOWARY

This dumpy, fluffy, flightless bird looks a bit comical, but don't be fooled! In Australia and New Guinea, where it lives, the cassowary is known as a seriously dangerous animal.

KILLER KICK

The cassowary is tall, strong, and has two deadly weapons—killer claws the size of a carrot, on each of its huge feet. It's also grumpy and highly territorial. If you invade its space, you're in trouble! When angry, a cassowary charges, hissing noisily. It jabs with its beak, or kicks and slashes with its claws. Sometimes, it even jumps up and kicks with both feet at once!

CAR-RIPPING CLAWS

A cassowary's claws are so strong and sharp, they can tear its victims open. One cassowary even ripped a hole in the side of a car! There's only one record of a cassowary killing a human, in 1926.

A close-up of a cassowary's foot showing its extra-large carrot-size claws.

DON'T FEED THE BIRDS

Some people feed wild cassowaries. This is a bad idea, as the birds learn to expect food from people, and start chasing after anyone they see. Heeelp!

DEADLY DEGREE

☠ ☠

Terrifying, but most humans are a match for the cassowary.

PITOHUI

In 1989, scientist Jack Dumbacher was scratched by a pitohui (*PIT-o-hooey*) bird while studying in Papua New Guinea. He put his sore hand in his mouth and felt a weird numbing sensation.

A pitohui, with its bright red feathers and hooded head.

FATAL FEATHERS

Experts found the pitohui's feathers and skin contain a poison called batrachotoxin (*ba-TRAK-o-toxin*). Luckily, there wasn't enough of it on Dumbacher's hand to kill him, although a small dose can kill a human. It's the same toxin found on poison dart frogs (see page 32). It paralyzes your muscles so you can't feel or move.

INSIDE KNOWLEDGE

Hooded pitohuis and the two other pitohui species, which are also poisonous, are common in Papua New Guinea. Local people avoid touching them. There are tales of people dying after brushing against a lot of pitohuis. Would you risk finding out if they're true?

STINKY BIRD

Besides being dangerous, and no use as food, the pitohui smells absolutely revolting. So local people have nicknamed it the "garbage bird."

DEADLY DEGREE

☠ ☠

It's deadly, but you're unlikely to encounter it.

OSTRICH

The world's biggest birds, the elephant bird and the giant moa, were as tall as an elephant! They are now extinct, but something similar survives today—the ostrich, the world's deadliest bird.

BIRD POWER

Ostriches can be much taller than an average human, at up to 8 feet (2.5 m). Like cassowaries (see page 24), they are mainly plant eaters. But, if an ostrich feels threatened or wants to protect its chicks, it will peck violently with its beak, and kick and slash so hard that it could kill a lion, or a human.

This farmer keeps 650 ostriches, and has to stay on his toes!

ROAD RUNNER

Ostriches can run at up to 44 mph (70 km/h), so they can easily outrun a human. One ostrich even chased a Jeep for several minutes, trying to peck at the passengers!

OSTRICH FARM FRENZY

Ostriches are often bred on farms for their meat, skin, and feathers. But farm ostriches are still wild animals and can be very bad-tempered, sometimes killing farmers.

DEADLY DEGREE

☠ ☠ ☠

An ostrich has a killer kick and a powerful peck.

EAGLE

Eagles are amazing creatures. They are huge, with a wingspan of up to 6.5 feet (2 m)—as wide as a couch. They have massive feet with sharp talons and beaks for tearing flesh.

A captive golden eagle turns nasty during a display.

HOW EAGLES HUNT

Eagles have brilliant eyesight, three to four times sharper than ours. They use it to find rabbits, birds, or other prey as they soar high above. When they spot a target, they plunge down with deadly accuracy, and grab it in their claws. They carry the victim away to their nest—or, if it's too big to lift, eat it on the ground.

COULD AN EAGLE EAT ME?

It's not impossible! Bald eagles, Philippine eagles, and Steller's sea eagles have been known to catch animals as big as deer. And huge harpy eagles in South America often catch monkeys and sloths. So, in theory, an eagle could catch a small human, though it's unlikely. But eagles do sometimes attack and claw at people to scare them away from their nests.

OH DEER!

In 2011, in Montana, a small deer was found dangling on a power line. Experts think an eagle caught it, carried it up high, then dropped it because it was too heavy.

DEADLY DEGREE

A deadly killer if you're a rabbit, but fairly safe for us.

KILLER REPTILES AND FIERCE FISH

You might not immediately think of fish as deadly—but think again! Dangerous fish include the humongous great white shark and the sneaky stonefish. Life-threatening reptiles, meanwhile, include terrifying crocodiles and slithery, venomous snakes.

KOMODO DRAGON

Sadly, no one has ever found a real dragon, so this is the closest thing we have. It doesn't have wings or breathe fire, but the Komodo dragon is a pretty amazing animal just the same.

TERRIBLE TRACKERS

The Komodo dragon is the biggest lizard on the planet, and is renowned for its ravenous, ferocious ways. Komodos are carnivores and will gobble up all kinds of food—even horses. A Komodo dragon can easily kill a human, too. One victim was picking fruit on an Indonesian island where the dragons live, when a group of Komodos tracked him down and ate him.

BITES, GERMS, AND VENOM

For a long time, scientists thought that deadly germs in the dragon's saliva killed its prey. Recently, they have found it actually injects venom, too. With its massive teeth and claws, the dragon can also kill some animals just by tearing them to bits.

DEADLY DEGREE

☠ ☠ ☠
✕ ✕ ✕

Komodo dragons are fierce carnivores.

A dragon makes quick work of its disgusting dinner with its giant jaws.

ONE ROTTING CORPSE, TO GO!

Besides hunting for prey, Komodo dragons also like to eat dead animals, and have been known to dig up human graves!

CROCODILE

There are lots of types of crocodiles, many of them deadly. But the deadliest of them all is the saltwater crocodile—also known as the estuarine crocodile, or "saltie."

DEATH ROLL

As their name suggests, salties can live in the sea. They also hang around in swamps, waiting until tasty prey approaches the shore. Then, a croc launches itself up, grabs its victim, and spins over in a "death roll" to pull the prey down. Lastly, the killer drags its meal underwater to gobble it up.

DEADLIEST CROC?

Saltwater crocodiles kill about two people a year in Australia. This croc also lives in India and Southeast Asia, where there are millions more people—so there are probably many unreported deaths. The saltie is the world's biggest reptile, reaching 23 feet (7 m) long and 2,200 pounds (1,000 kg) in weight. A big one could stretch across a classroom!

HUNGRY HUNTER

Crocs don't just attack if they're annoyed. They kill for food. Some victims are never found because they're in the croc's stomach.

DEADLY DEGREE

Once a crocodile grabs its prey, there's no escape.

Imagine being caught in these giant, gruesome jaws!

AMERICAN ALLIGATOR

The American alligator has the most powerful bite measured in any animal. Its jaws snap shut as hard as a car falling on top of you! But would an alligator eat us?

SEE YOU LATER, ALLIGATOR!

Though not as big as a saltwater crocodile, an American alligator is a chunky, powerful predator. As well as feeding on fish and turtles, it will snap up any land creature that comes too close to the water's edge—which has included a few humans. Besides having a big bite, an alligator can also use its mighty tail to whack you and knock you down.

MONSTER OF THE SWAMPS

American alligators live in the southern United States, mainly Florida and Louisiana. They lurk in swampy areas such as the Florida Everglades. The alligator is the United States' biggest reptile. They are around 11 feet (3.5 m) long, but a large male can reach a giant 18 feet (5.5 m). Alligator moms are most dangerous when defending their babies.

An alligator wrestles with its prey.

SLIMY, SCARY SURPRISE

There could be an alligator in any waterway in the southern United States. Most victims are attacked while swimming!

DEADLY DEGREE

☠ ☠ ☠

A deadly hunter with a brutal bite.

POISON DART FROG

Who's scared of tiny frogs? Well, if you're not, you should be! Poison dart frogs have deadly poisons in their skin. These are sometimes so powerful it can be dangerous even to touch them.

THE DEATHLY DART

Local people in the jungles of South and Central America collect poison from the frogs' skin and dip their blowpipe darts into it. A hunter blows the darts through a hollow tube to kill animals. Hunters use only a few species of poison frogs, including the deadliest of all, the golden dart frog.

DON'T TOUCH

A single golden dart frog has enough paralyzing poison in it to kill up to 20 adults. You really could die just from touching its skin—and this is said to have happened in the past. However, it's quite unlikely, as this frog is rare and endangered.

The strawberry poison dart frog is not as sweet as it sounds!

DEADLY DEGREE

One of the most poisonous animals on our planet.

STAY AWAY FROM ME!

The poison puts off predators that try to eat the frogs. The frogs' amazing bright red, yellow, blue, or green markings act as a warning that they are toxic.

BUSHMASTER

This snake's scientific name, *Lachesis muta*, means "silent fate." It's a killer pit viper that can sneak around without a sound. In the South American jungle, everyone fears the enormous, deadly bushmaster.

SNEAKY SNAKE

Although it's big, the bushmaster is great at slipping slowly and quietly through the undergrowth. It stalks prey such as mice, rats, and agoutis (large rodents a little like guinea pigs). Or it may lie coiled up for days, waiting for prey to pass by. This means that people sometimes accidentally disturb or tread on a bushmaster. And when it's surprised or annoyed, the snake strikes fast, with its long, supersharp fangs.

The bushmaster's fangs can reach 1.5 inches (3.5 cm) in length.

EATEN ALIVE

The bushmaster's venom isn't the strongest in the world, but the viper injects a lot of it, and it has VERY nasty effects. It damages blood vessels, and quickly starts to digest and dissolve living flesh. Ugh! Victims can be left with a deep craterlike wound, or may even have to have their arm or leg amputated—that's if they survive!

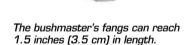
DEADLY DEGREE

Luckily, it's unlikely you will bump into a bushmaster.

WHAT'S PIT ALL ABOUT?

Pit vipers are venomous snakes that have a pair of special heat-sensing organs, or "heat pits," on their faces. They use these pits to detect the body heat of their prey.

INLAND TAIPAN

Australia's inland taipan isn't as famous as other deadly snakes. Maybe you haven't even heard of it. But it has the deadliest venom of any land snake!

SIGNAL PROBLEMS

Inland taipan venom is so powerful, one bite's worth could kill over 100 people. It contains several killer chemicals. One stops your nerves from working, so your brain can't send messages to your body. You can't move, your vision blurs, and eventually you can't even breathe! One chemical eats away at your muscles and another stops your blood from clotting, so you bleed to death. Yikes!

THE GOOD NEWS

Luckily, the inland taipan is very shy. It eats only small animals and hides from humans. Some people do get bitten—usually scientists who are trying to catch the snakes and study them. But there is an antivenom that can save them.

FAST FANGS

The taipan strikes very fast and hard, so when it bites, its fangs sink in a long way. The venom is injected deep into the victim's flesh, so it works fast.

DEADLY DEGREE

☠ ☠ ☠ ☠ ☠
✕ ✕ ✕ ✕ ✕

The inland taipan's bite is one of the world's most lethal.

An inland taipan prepares to strike its prey in the Australian desert.

INDIAN COBRA

A cobra rearing up, with its hood spread out, is one of the scariest snake scenarios most people can imagine. Indian cobras make this display as a warning, before they strike.

A cobra spreads out its wide hood ready to fight a mongoose.

SIGNS OF A BITE

The Indian cobra can bite its chosen victim several times, injecting a lot of venom. Cobras have also been known to hold on to their victims and chew them. At first, the venom makes your eyelids droop and your tongue numb. It damages cells, making the poison spread through the body faster. When it reaches the heart or lungs, they stop working. A bite can kill a human in one hour.

HERE, THERE, AND EVERYWHERE

Indian cobras are common across India. They often appear in yards, farm fields, and in houses, where they go in search of mice and rats to eat. Thousands of people get bitten every year, and many of them die. There is a treatment available, but a lot of people don't get it in time.

DEADLY DEGREE

☠ ☠ ☠ ☠

One of the deadliest of India's many terrifying snakes.

CHARMING!

Snake charmers make their cobras "dance" by playing a tune on a pipe. In fact, snakes can't hear music, but they follow the movement of the pipe and feel the vibrations from the charmer tapping his foot.

RETICULATED PYTHON

If the picture on this page doesn't give you a scare, nothing will! This is a reticulated python, the longest snake in the world, devouring a whole deer. It's deadly, but not because of its bite.

SNAKE SNACKS

Pythons are constrictor snakes. They coil around their prey, squeeze it so hard it can't breathe, then swallow it whole. The creatures a python can swallow depend on the size of the python. Smaller pythons eat rats and birds; bigger ones can devour monkeys or pigs. And the biggest reticulated pythons, which can reach 26–30 feet (8–9 m) long, can eat a bear, a goat—or a human. However, this is very rare.

PEOPLE-EATING PYTHONS?

There have been a handful of reports of human bodies being found inside wild pythons. And, because some people keep them as pets, they have occasionally squeezed their owners to death.

DEADLY DEGRE

☠ ☠

Not terribly deadly, as it's rar for a constrictor to harm a hum

Look away or you might lose your appetite! It's feeding time for this pyt

NARROW ESCAPE

A naughty pet python wrapped itself around a three-year-old boy in 2009. Thankfully, his mom managed to fight the snake off.

BOOMSLANG

The boomslang is a very odd snake. It's unrelated to most killer snakes, and it doesn't look like them, either. But you still need to watch out for its lethal bite. . . .

THERE'S ONLY ONE BOOMSLANG!

It's easy to identify a boomslang, as it's so unique. First, it has enormous eyes—bigger for its size than any other snake—and it can see in color. Snakes normally detect their prey by scent, body heat, or movement. But the boomslang's big eyes can see prey that's sitting still. It can even spot a camouflaged chameleon!

THE BOOMSLANG'S BITE

The boomslang's fangs aren't at the front of its mouth, as in most snakes—they're at the back. It has to open its mouth superwide to bite. Its deadly venom is also unusual—it destroys the body's red blood cells. The bite can be treated, but if it isn't, the unlucky victim can bleed to death.

This boomslang has got its eye on you—beware!

DEADLY DEGREE

☠ ☠

Rarely deadly, but if you do get bitten, it's a horrible way to go.

PUFFED UP WARNING

Look out for a boomslang that has an inflated neck— this means it's about to strike. Move away fast!

MAMBA

A mamba is a venomous snake that scares the living daylights out of people in Africa, its home. All mambas are venomous, but the most famous and deadly is the black mamba.

The black mamba gets it name from the dark black inside of its mouth.

SUPER-SNAKE

This is the longest snake in Africa, growing up to 13 feet (4 m) in length. It's also the world's fastest snake! It can race along at 12 mph (20 km/h)—as fast as you might go on a bicycle. It can also raise its front half right up in the air, to climb up into a tree or to look around for potential victims.

THE WANDERER

Unlike other mambas, which stay in the trees, the black mamba often slithers along the ground. So it's more likely to meet humans, especially farm workers in the fields. The mamba will escape if it can, but if it's cornered, it strikes suddenly. Its deadly venom makes the muscles freeze up, and the heart and lungs stop working.

CALL AN AMBULANCE!

In the past, being bitten by a black mamba meant certain death in just 20 minutes! But there is now an antivenom, so if a victim gets to hospital quickly, they can be saved.

DEADLY DEGREE

☠ ☠ ☠

This snake has killer venom and strikes superfast.

RUSSELL'S VIPER

Some snakes have deadlier venom, many are bigger and more aggressive. But the Russell's viper, a brown snake common in India, China, and Southeast Asia, probably kills the most people.

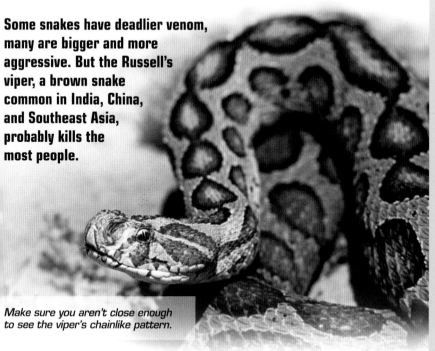

Make sure you aren't close enough to see the viper's chainlike pattern.

DEADLY FACTORS

Thousands of people die each year from Russell's viper bites. Why?

• The Russell's viper lives in highly populated areas.

• It invades homes and villages to find rats and mice to eat.

• It also hangs out in rice fields, where farmers work.

• It's well-camouflaged.

• It can come out in day or night.

• It's usually slow and quiet, but if disturbed, it gets upset and suddenly hisses, coils up, springs, and bites.

• It's chunky and strong, so not very easy to fight off.

• Its venom causes a lot of problems, like blood poisoning and organ failure. These problems are hard to treat, even in the hospital.

HISSSSSS!

Your main warning that you've annoyed a deadly Russell's viper is its sudden, noisy hiss. It is said to have the loudest hiss of any snake.

DEADLY DEGREE

Keep a close eye out for this stealthy snake.

AUSTRALIAN BROWN SNAKE

Names don't get much more boring than "brown snake." But this snake is seriously scary. Its venom is extremely lethal, and it's not afraid to bite anyone who bothers it.

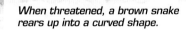

DEADLY DEGREE

☠ ☠ ☠ ☠ ☠
✕ ✕ ✕ ✕ ✕

Lethal venom and a lot of bites make this snake very deadly indeed

OUT OF VENOM

Around 3,000 people get bitten by snakes each year in Australia, up to half of them by brown snakes. But sometimes they are lucky and get a "dry bite" with no venom.

When threatened, a brown snake rears up into a curved shape.

DEADLY EFFECTS

The brown snake's venom prevents blood from clotting and body organs from working. It can even make victims collapse in a coma. Some other snakes, like the inland taipan (see page 34), have deadlier venom. But the brown snake is Australia's number one killer snake, as it's often found around human homes—and it's not afraid to bite.

SPEEDY SLITHERER

Brown snakes are about 5 feet (1.5 m) long, slender, and attack quickly. Their bite isn't very painful, and may sometimes not hurt at all. Sounds good? It's not! It means that people sometimes don't notice they've been bitten until it's too late. There is an antivenom that can treat them, but victims can die if they don't get help in time.

DEATH ADDER

Imagine you're a bird foraging in the undergrowth, when you spot a tasty worm. You grab it and—BAM! Before you know it, you're on a one-way journey down a death adder's throat!

Check out how tiny the death adder's "tail" is, compared to its body.

WHAT HAPPENED?

The death adder plays a sneaky trick on its prey. Its wide, chunky body narrows to a tiny tip that looks like a worm. The snake hides under dead leaves with only this tail sticking out to attract birds or lizards. When they come close enough, the death adder strikes! Humans also end up getting bitten, because they don't see the snake and so they step on it.

LIGHTNING STRIKE

The death adder is said to strike faster than any other snake—it can go from motionless to having a mouthful of prey in less than a fifth of a second. Its venom can take several hours to kill a human, so there's usually time to get treatment. But, before a cure was invented, half of all its victims died.

DEADLY DEGREE

☠️ ☠️ ☠️

Dangerous, but most bites are no longer fatal.

DEAF ADDER?

Unlike most snakes, which avoid people, the death adder doesn't seem to notice when humans are around—so it has the nickname "deaf adder." Maybe it stays put to wait for unsuspecting prey.

BEAKED SEA SNAKE

Some of the deadliest snakes don't live on land—they swim in the sea, swishing along with a paddle-like tail. The beaked sea snake of the Indian Ocean is one of the most feared.

DON'T MESS WITH ME!

It seems strange to call a wild animal mean—but fishermen, scientists, and reptile experts all agree that the beaked sea snake is seriously bad-tempered. It is quick to bite anyone who disturbs it. It also attacks people who haven't bothered it at all. Along with its venom, this is what makes this sea snake so deadly.

SNEAKY BITE

The beaked sea snake's bite hardly hurts at all. It can bite its victims and be gone before they notice. Its venom isn't quite as strong as some other snakes', but one bite contains a lot—enough to kill 50 people. The poison makes victims feel stiff and achy at first. Eventually, their muscles start to dissolve. Horrible!

Imagine getting tangled up with this snake during a swim.

BEAKED BITES

Experts think this sea serpent is responsible for half of all sea snake bites, and nine out of ten sea snake deaths.

DEADLY DEGREE

A hot contender for the title of world's deadliest snake!

ELECTRIC EEL

Electricity seems like something hi-tech. But it's not—it's part of nature. Some animals can even generate their own electricity to use as a weapon. The most powerful of all is the electric eel.

IT'S A SHOCKER!

Most of the electric eel's body is filled with organs that work like batteries to build up an electric charge. The eel releases the electrical energy in a powerful pulse. It uses the charge to stun its prey, such as fish and crustaceans, and also to fight off hungry hunters, like crocodiles.

CAN IT KILL?

A power socket in your house can be deadly—but an electric eel can deliver a shock up to five times more powerful than that. The eel's shock is very short—less than a second—and wouldn't usually kill a human. But getting several shocks could stop the heart.

DEADLY DEGREE

Unlikely to kill, but this eel packs a deadly weapon.

ZAP . . . OUCH!

Why doesn't the electric eel electrocute itself? Good question! Its skin is thick and resistant to electricity. The electrical current flows more easily through to the eel's prey than to the eel itself—so that's where it goes!

The gruesome electric eel can reach over 6.5 feet (2 m) long.

TIGER SHARK

Once a tiger shark gets a sniff of food, it becomes frighteningly fierce. These sharks will eat almost any kind of prey. To them, a swimmer is probably just another snack to try!

SHALLOW SWIM

Tiger sharks are known for their ravenous hunger and trash can-style approach to eating. They swim in shallow water, close to the seashore, where they can be a deadly risk to humans.

I'LL EAT ANYTHING!

Some unbelievable items have been found in tiger sharks' stomachs—including:
- Old oil drum
- Glass bottles
- Rubber tire
- Cushion
- Baseball
- Human hand—eek!

SURFING SURVIVOR

In 2003, 13-year-old Bethany Hamilton was attacked by a tiger shark while surfing in Hawaii. It bit her left arm off completely!

A tiger shark lurks in the shallow waters of the Bahamas.

DEADLY DEGREE

You don't want to bump into a tiger shark when going for a dip.

GREAT WHITE SHARK

Think of a deadly creature and a shark is sure to spring to mind! Thanks to scary movies, stories, and sailors' tales, there are few animals people fear more. But how deadly are they really?

GREAT WHITE TEETH

The great white is the biggest hunting shark, growing up to 23 feet (7 m) long, and it has rows of huge, terrifying teeth. It uses them to bite to bits all kinds of ocean prey such as seals, squid, penguins, dolphins, and even turtles. Experts think sharks don't actually like the taste of humans much, and eat only us when they mistake us for something else, like a sea lion.

DEADLY DEGREE

Not quite as deadly as it might seem, luckily!

SHARK ON BOARD!

In 2011, a great white landed on a boat full of scientists doing a shark study! They were OK—but on a smaller boat, this could have been deadly.

A great white desperate to get into a shark-spotter's cage.

BULL SHARK

The great white shark has a scary reputation, and you might think it's the deadliest shark there is. But beware of the bull!

BIG BURLY BULLS

Bull sharks are a bit smaller than great whites, but they are fiercer and lurk in shallow waters. In fact, experts think bull sharks probably kill more people than any other type of shark. Like real bulls, they are strong, sturdy, and chunky. They're also easily annoyed, and will deliberately attack people—unlike most sharks, which are shy.

HANGING AROUND HUMANS

One reason bull sharks are deadly is that they often go near humans. Unusual for sharks, they also swim a long way up rivers. In the Ganges River in India, bull sharks are a danger to people bathing or washing clothes. They have also been found an incredible 2,500 miles (4,000 km) up the Amazon River in South America.

You can tell a bull shark by its thick, heavy body and stubby snout.

DEADLY DEGREE

As sharks go, this is the deadliest.

SHARK BAIT

To avoid becoming a bull shark's breakfast, don't swim in river mouths or wide rivers in warm, tropical parts of the world.

GOLIATH TIGER FISH

This fearsome fish is a legend among fishermen. There are many tales of it leaping onto boats, biting people, and fighting viciously. But is it really a killer?

DEADLY DEGREE

Looks amazingly deadly—but actually doesn't eat people.

This giant goliath tiger fish could easily fit your head in its mouth!

RIVER TIGER

The goliath tiger fish is one of the world's biggest fish, at up to 6.5 feet (2 m) long, and some say one of the fiercest. But it's not a shark and it doesn't even live in the sea—it's found in the Congo River, in Africa. Local people say it's the only fish that doesn't fear the crocodiles, and it's even said to bite them! As you can see, it has some seriously scary teeth, which can be even bigger than a great white shark's—and it could give you a very nasty bite. However, there aren't many reliable reports of attacks. One fisherman is said to have been bitten badly on his side, but he was stitched up.

TERRIBLE TEETH

The tiger fish's teeth are so razor-sharp, they could slice through skin, and snap off a finger or a whole hand in a second. Some reports say they can bite through steel wire!

STONEFISH

Is it a stone? Is it a coral? Is it a lump of seaweed? No, it's a fish, and whatever you do, DON'T stand on it! This is the stonefish, the world's most venomous fish.

LINE OF SPINES

The stonefish has bumpy skin and can change color to match the rocks around it on the seabed. It also has 13 sharp, deadly spines along its back. They stick up if the stonefish feels threatened. If anything touches the fish's back, the spines inject their venom.

OOOOWWWWWW!

A stonefish sting is incredibly painful. It can also paralyze you, make it hard to breathe, or even make you fall unconscious (not good when you're knee-deep in water!). Without help, the sting can be deadly within two hours.

DEADLY DEGREE

Wins the award for having the deadliest venom of any fish!

A stonefish is hard to spot on the seabed. Up close you can see its face

JUST CUT IT OFF!

A stonefish sting hurts so much, it's said some victims have begged to have their foot cut off!

PUFFER FISH

When a puffer fish is scared, it sucks in water (or air) and "puffs" up into a ball shape. By inflating itself, it can make itself much bigger, and almost impossible for a predator to eat.

POISONOUS PUFFER

The puffer fish's puffing isn't dangerous, but it does have a secret weapon—its body contains a deadly poison called tetrodotoxin *(TE-trod-o-TOX-in)*.

DEADLY DINNER

In Japanese restaurants, where they are known as *fugu*, puffer fish are a great delicacy! They are prepared by specially trained chefs. A *fugu* chef removes most

DEADLY DEGREE

☠ ☠ ☠ ☠ ☠
✕ ✕ ✕ ✕ ✕

It's incredibly poisonous, yet people eat it on purpose!

of the poison, leaving just enough to give the diner an exciting tingly feeling around the mouth.

A puffer fish in the sea, blowing itself up from slim to spherical.

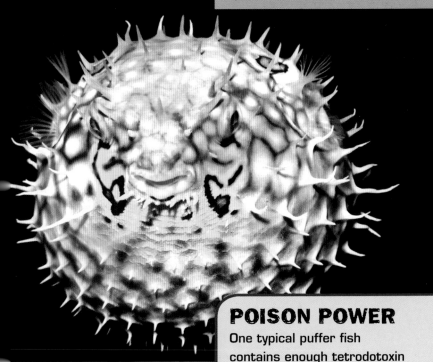

POISON POWER

One typical puffer fish contains enough tetrodotoxin to kill about 30 people!

NEEDLEFISH

The needlefish gets its name from its long needlelike snout or "beak." Needlefish grow to only around 3 feet (1 m) long. Yet, they can be very dangerous, thanks to their strange behavior.

A school of needlefish darts through the water at incredible speed.

FLYING DAGGERS
Look out! Needlefish often leap out of the water and through the air at speeds of up to 35 mph (55 km/h). They do this to avoid danger, but will also jump over small boats rather than swim around them. They are attracted to light, too. So people who fish at night, with lights on their boat, can suddenly be hit by a needlefish flinging itself through the air, like a deadly dagger.

ACCIDENTAL ATTACK
Needlefish don't mean to attack people, but they can cause serious injuries, and even some deaths. Some victims have had to be rescued and airlifted to a hospital after being stabbed in the back or head. Even worse, the fish's beak can break off and get stuck inside your body. Oww!

FLYING COUSINS
Needlefish are closely related to real flying fish, which explains their leaping habits. However, they don't have the large, winglike fins that help flying fish stay in the air longer.

DEADLY DEGREE
☠
Not a major risk, but a flying needlefish is best avoided!

STINGRAY

It's the excruciating sting in the tail that gives the stingray its name. Its tail is a long spine that can stab the ray's enemies and inject unbelievably painful venom.

BOTTOM-FEEDER

Stingrays have wide, flat bodies, with the mouth on the underside. They cruise along the bottom of seas or rivers, munching on prey like shellfish and shrimp. To hide from danger, a stingray wriggles into the mud or sand, with just its eyes showing. If something swims over it, or steps on it, its tail suddenly flicks up and forward, and the spine jabs into whatever, or whoever, is in the way.

STEPPING ON A SPINE

Most victims get stung on the foot and, though this REALLY hurts—the venom can destroy your foot—it isn't strong enough to kill you. But if the sting enters the body or head, damaging an important organ, it can be fatal.

DEADLY DEGREE

Stingrays are not out to get us, and very rarely kill.

A stealthy stingray hunts for a suitable hiding place.

STEVE IRWIN

TV naturalist Steve Irwin died in 2006, when he was stabbed in the chest by a stingray. This has made some people scared of stingrays—but Irwin was just very unlucky.

BLOODTHIRSTY BEASTIES

Although creepy crawlies are little, many people are more scared of them than anything else. Spiders, in particular, are the stuff of nightmares, and some of them can be seriously deadly. So can many kinds of flies, ants, jellyfish, and other invertebrates—either because of their killer bites and stings, or the deadly diseases they spread.

BLUE-RINGED OCTOPUS

You might think of a deadly octopus as a giant sea monster, gobbling up divers or wrapping its tentacles around passing ships. But the real-life deadliest octopus is tiny—smaller than this book.

BLUE-RING WARNING

If you see an octopus like this, don't touch it! Actually, the blue-ringed octopus has blue rings only when it's annoyed and about to bite. The rest of the time it camouflages itself against the rocks or seabed, as octopuses are able to change color.

BEAKY BITE!

If you do bother this octopus, or accidentally step on it, it will bite with its sharp beak and inject deadly venom. The venom is strong—one octopus has enough to kill more than 20 people. It paralyzes its victims' muscles, so they can't breathe. That means certain death, unless you can get to a hospital where a life-support machine can breathe for you. Then, once the venom wears off, you'll be OK.

Watch out for an octopus with these electric-blue rings.

CRAB-CRUNCHING BEAKS

An octopus's hard, beak-shaped mouth helps it eat hard-shelled prey such as crabs. The beak is found right in the middle of the long tentacles.

DEADLY DEGREE

☠☠☠☠☠
✕✕✕✕✕

One of the world's tiniest, deadliest creatures.

BOX JELLYFISH

If you want to know what a truly deadly creature looks like—here it is! The box jellyfish has the deadliest sting of any animal. One touch from its trailing tentacles can kill. . . .

A box jellyfish propels itself through the water.

JELLY VENOM

The jellyfish's 6-foot (2-m) long tentacles are covered in thousands of tiny stingers, called nematocysts. If they touch another animal, they shoot out microscopic darts, injecting their venom in a fraction of a second. This venom can stop the heart. A sting from just one of the jellyfish's many tentacles can kill a human in three minutes. Around the Pacific and Indian Oceans, dozens die every year from box jellyfish stings.

LOOK OUT!

Unfortunately for swimmers, the box jelly, as it is sometimes called, is very hard to see in the water, as its squarish, box-shaped top is almost completely clear.

STAYING ALIVE

In Australia, some beaches have underwater nets around them to stop jellyfish getting in, and bottles of vinegar to treat stings. Victims can survive if they are doused with vinegar, the tentacles are pulled off, and they are rushed to the hospital.

DEADLY DEGREE

One of the world's most venomous creatures.

PORTUGUESE MAN-OF-WAR

Like a jellyfish, a Portuguese man-of-war has horribly painful, stinging tentacles that leave red stripe marks when they sting you. But this odd creature is not really a jellyfish. . . .

TENTACLE TANGLE

A man-of-war is actually a colony, or group of living things that work together as a whole. Some catch food, some eat, some reproduce, and some help the colony move. A man-of-war drifts along on the ocean surface, thanks to its bright blue, gas-filled, floating "sail," which is up to 1 foot (30 cm) across. The man-of-war has no brain and can't decide where to go—it just floats where the wind blows it. Its tentacles can be 40 feet (12 m) long. They can tangle around swimmers' arms or legs, and cling as they inject their venom. Ouch!

It's a good thing men-of-war just float along. We can stay clear.

PAINFUL—BUT DEADLY?

The man-of-war's sting is painful and scary, and it has been known to kill people. Out at sea, the pain can make people panic and end up drowning. In rare cases, the venom damages the heart or causes an allergic shock—especially if someone is unlucky enough to be stung by a lot of men-of-war at once. To avoid Portuguese men-of-war, stay clear of the sea when the wind is blowing toward the shore—this deadly creature may have blown in!

STOLEN STINGERS

The tentacles can still sting you after the man-of-war is dead, or after the tentacles have been pulled off. One type of octopus even pulls them off the man-of-war and uses them to sting its own enemies!

DEADLY DEGREE

Weird-looking, but rarely a killer.

CONE SHELL

You may have seen beautiful, cone-shaped seashells in seaside stores. They're safe because there's no animal inside. But in the sea, these sneaky creatures carry terrifyingly deadly weapons.

DEADLY DART

The cone shell, or cone snail, preys on other sea creatures such as fish. It injects them with powerful venom, using a long, supersharp dart that reaches out of its shell. Once the prey is helpless, the snail stretches out its enormous, trumpet-shaped mouth and wraps it around the prey to digest it. Mmmm!

KILLER CONE

Cone snails can kill humans, too, although they're not large enough to actually eat us. Their deadly venom is made up of over 100 different chemicals, and there is no antivenom for it. It's especially dangerous as people often pick this snail up to admire its amazing shell.

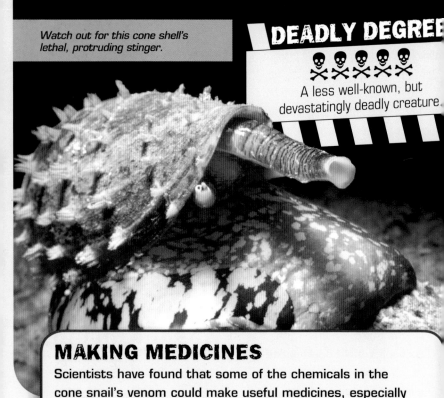

Watch out for this cone shell's lethal, protruding stinger.

DEADLY DEGREE

A less well-known, but devastatingly deadly creature.

MAKING MEDICINES

Scientists have found that some of the chemicals in the cone snail's venom could make useful medicines, especially painkillers. They are working on making copies of these chemicals in science labs.

FLATWORM

Flatworms are a large family of creatures that mostly look like what they sound like—flat worms! But they're not harmless. In fact, they have a lot of ways to cause trouble.

FLAT AND FEARSOME

Here are just a few of flatworms' mischievous methods:

• Flatworms known as liver flukes get into people's skin when they swim in infected water. They cause a long-lasting illness called bilharzia, which can be deadly.

• Some flatworms, called tapeworms, can get into humans if people eat meat from an infected animal. The worms live inside your intestines, and grow longer and longer as they feed on your food.

• Some flatworms can even invade your brain and fill it with lumplike cysts—eww!

• Others live on their own in the ocean. They release a revolting snotlike substance, which puts predators off eating them.

A bilharzia sufferer has a painful, swollen abdomen.

DEADLY DEGREE

Flatworms make life miserable for millions of people in poor countries.

DID YOU KNOW?

A tapeworm living inside a human can grow a segmented chainlike body up to 65 feet (20 m) long—that's longer than a fire truck!

MOSQUITO

One of the smallest animals is also the deadliest. Mosquitoes are less than 0.75 inches (2 cm) long, and sometimes you can't even see them—but these mini germ-spreaders kill millions.

DISASTROUS DISEASES

A mosquito bite itself isn't dangerous—it just gives you an itchy spot. Mosquitoes are deadly because they can spread killer diseases, including malaria, yellow fever, and dengue (*Den-gay*) fever. The mosquito carries the germs in its body, and when it bites, they pass into its victim. Malaria is the deadliest mosquito-spread disease—around a million people die from it every year.

BLOOD FOR BABIES

Mosquitoes don't actually feed on blood most of the time. But when a female is ready to lay eggs, she bites someone and sucks their blood to get the iron and protein she needs—and leaves you with a nasty, painful bite.

A mosquito's body brimming over with human blood.

DEADLY DEGREE

This buzzing, biting bug is the biggest killer on the planet.

SNIFFING YOU OUT

Mosquitoes can track down humans from up to 160 feet (50 m) away by the special smell of our sweat!

TSETSE FLY

If this big, fat, biting bug from Africa sucks your blood, you could end up with sleeping sickness. It may not sound that bad, but it's actually one of the world's deadliest—and nastiest—diseases.

NOT-SO-SLEEPING SICKNESS

As the tsetse fly feeds, it spreads sleeping sickness from one person, or animal, to the next. If you catch the disease, you get aches and pains, a fever, and horrible itching. Then, you start to feel incredibly weak and tired. As the disease gets worse, it drives people crazy, until they finally die. There is a medicine that can cure sleeping sickness, but for many people, it's too expensive. So hundreds of thousands of unlucky victims die each year.

FOOD FOR LIFE

Sleeping sickness also affects farm animals, such as cows. When they get the disease, it's called "nagana." They can't provide milk or have calves. It's a deadly disaster for farmers if their animals catch nagana, as they lose their food supply and their living selling milk.

DID YOU KNOW?

In a single feeding session, a tsetse fly can drink twice its own weight in blood. It's amazing that it can still fly away afterward!

The tsetse feeds with its extra-long, snoutlike mouth.

DEADLY DEGREE

Not quite as bad news as the mosquito, but definitely dangerous.

LOCUST

Did you know that grasshoppers can be deadly? Locusts are a strange type of grasshopper that suddenly gather into scary swarms. But why do they do this? What makes it deadly?

TRANSFORMERS

Scientists have found that locusts switch to swarming mode when they run out of food, and end up crowded together, fighting for a few plants. Jostling against one another prompts them to form a swarm. They collect into a huge cloud, or "locust storm," and set off in search of food. Usually, that means unlucky farmers' crops. The locusts descend on the fields and strip them bare. They eat so much food, they leave nothing for humans, who can then starve to death.

A boy is caught up in a raging locust swarm in Africa.

HUNGRY KILLER

Each locust can devour its own body weight in vegetation every day, and a medium-sized locust swarm can eat as much food in a day as 100,000 people.

ASIAN GIANT HORNET

Nobody likes a wasp buzzing around them. But imagine if it was as big as the Asian giant hornet—the biggest wasp in the world.

A close-up of the giant hornet's enormous jaws. And look at it munching on that bee!

BZZZZZ!

This hornet has a big sting, and can sting you several times. The venom is actually less toxic than a killer bee's (see page 62), but there's a lot more of it, so stings are deadlier. The pain is like being stabbed by a burning-hot nail. Even worse, the hornet sometimes bites you with its massive jaws at the same time. Nasty!

IS THE HORNET DEADLY?

It can be. Most people recover, but some have a sudden allergic reaction. And, rarely, the venom can cause breathing and heart problems, especially if someone is stung many times. Since these hornets live in nests and can swarm, that's not unheard of.

SCARY STINGS

These bugs cause about 40 deaths per year. In Japan, where the hornet is common, it's the deadliest wild animal of all—even worse than a brown bear.

DEADLY DEGREE

☠ ☠ ☠
✖ ✖ ✖

A surprisingly serious threat.

KILLER BEE

A beesting is not nice. It hurts a lot, and can swell up into a sore, itchy lump. But surely bees aren't THAT bad! So what are they doing in this book!?

KILLER BEES!
Killer bees sound like something from a cartoon, but they're a real problem. They look almost exactly like normal bees. But they are a special variety, known as Africanized bees, bred by accident in the 1950s. Unlike normal bees, they become angry easily, chase people, and attack in a swarm.

ALLERGIC REACTION
Just one beesting can be deadly, if the person who is stung is allergic to it. Let alone the effects of an attack from a swarm of Africanized bees—they have been known to chase people a quarter of a mile (0.4 km). They actually kill more humans than many wild animals, like tigers and wolves.

A beekeeper lets himself be covered in bees to break a world record— a swarm this size could be fatal.

DEADLY DEGREE

Usually won't bother you—but there are exceptions!

HIGH-SPEED BEES

A swarm of killer bees (and normal bees, too) can fly along at up to 12 mph (20 km/h). Most people can't run that fast!

TICK

There are few things more disgusting than having a fat, squishy tick on your leg. It buries its head in your skin, then grows and grows as it sucks your blood. Ewww!

DEADLY DISEASES

Ticks aren't just gross. Their bites spread some seriously nasty diseases, too. The most famous is Lyme disease. It starts with a rash, and then feels a bit like a flu. But if it's not treated, it can get much worse, and end up being fatal. Some victims go insane, and some become paralyzed. There are other killer diseases spread by ticks, too, such as babesiosis (*bab-e-SI-o-sis*), which destroys blood cells.

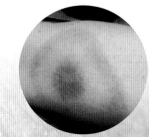

A ring-shaped rash like this is an early sign of Lyme disease.

WHERE ARE THEY FROM?

Ticks are little, bloodsucking creepy crawlies, related to spiders. They hang around in woodlands and long grass, and when a person or animal brushes past, they cling to them and start feeding. Sometimes they attach themselves to pets, who then bring them indoors!

A disgusting close-up of a dog tick in human skin.

DEADLY DEGREE

☠ ☠

ks cause a number of diseases, some of them fatal.

TICK CHECK!

People who live or hike in areas that have ticks should check for them when they get home. If they find one on their body, they have to pull it off carefully, with tweezers, making sure they don't squish it—that could squeeze dangerous germs out of the tick.

DEATHSTALKER SCORPION

As its name suggests, this is a scorpion you do not want to meet on a dark night. It's thought to have the deadliest venom of any scorpion, and it's not friendly, either!

SO YELLOW!

The deathstalker is also called the yellow scorpion. It can be such a bright yellow or yellowish-green color, some people say it looks like a plastic toy scorpion, at first glance.

DEADLY DEGREE

Several scorpions are deadly, but this one takes the cake.

A yellow deathstalker would be well-camouflaged in its home, the deserts of the Middle East.

SUPER STINGER

This scorpion is small, but able to defend itself, and stings easily. Being kept in captivity makes it even more jumpy and nervous, and more likely to attack. Like the fat-tailed scorpion (opposite), it doesn't kill everyone it stings. The sting is horrendously painful, and damages the heart— so people with weak hearts are especially at risk.

SPOT THE DEADLY SCORPION

To tell how dangerous a scorpion is, look at its claws. If they're big and strong, that means it uses them for hunting, and doesn't need much venom. If they're small and spindly—beware! That means it has a powerful sting to capture prey.

FAT-TAILED SCORPION

Some scorpions reach over 8 inches (20 cm) long—larger than this book! Though they look scary, smaller scorpions, like the fat-tailed scorpion, are actually the deadliest ones.

FAT-TAILED MAN KILLER

There are several types of fat-tailed scorpion, all sharing the Latin name *Androctonus*, meaning "man killer." The wide, strong

DEADLY DEGREE

☠ ☠ ☠ ☠

One of the most deadliest scorpions in the world.

A scorpion, about to sting, curls its tail forward over its back.

tail isn't just powerful—it also contains a large store of deadly venom. The scorpion's sting is agonizing, and can make you dizzy, numb, and breathless. A healthy adult should survive, but children, the elderly, and anyone who's sick might not be so lucky.

HIDING IN YOUR BED!

Fat-tailed scorpions go hunting at night, and rest in the daytime. They like to find a nice, dark hiding place—like under a stone, or in your boot or sleeping bag! If anyone disturbs or squashes them, they go on the attack.

SCORPION SPEED

A fat-tailed scorpion can move frighteningly fast—especially when it's warm. Luckily for us, as the temperature falls, the scorpion becomes sluggish, so it's easier to escape its sting!

AFRICAN SAFARI ANT

It can be annoying when a trail of hungry ants finds its way into your kitchen. So imagine millions and millions of them, marching right through your house in a massive swarm!

SMALL BUT DEADLY

In Africa, safari ants live together in huge groups, or colonies. Their favorite food is fresh meat. If the local supply starts to run out, they surge through the forest in a big, long trail, or "column," killing and devouring any living thing that's in their way. Working together, the ants can kill animals much bigger than themselves. They swarm over them and nibble them into pieces.

GET OUT OF THE WAY!

Marching safari ants can be deadly to humans. If you get caught in an ant column, there's a risk of being suffocated or bitten to death. However, we can run faster than the ants can march, so it's usually easy to avoid them.

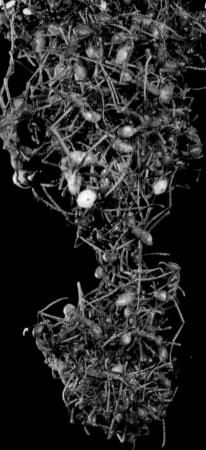

African safari ants create a bridge by joining their toes together.

DEADLY DEGREE

A deadly force of nature, but keep out of the way and you'll be OK.

SEEING BY SMELLING

Safari ants are blind, so they can't even see where they're marching! They communicate through touch and by releasing smelly chemical signals.

FIRE ANT

Fire ants get their name because of the burning pain of their stings. The imported red fire ant comes from South America, but has spread to other places including the United States and China.

ATTACKING ARMY

If fire ants are annoyed, they swarm out of their nest to attack. Each fire ant grabs your skin with its jaws to get a good grip, then uses the sting on its tail to inject its painful venom. It can move its bottom end around to sting you several times. Each sting swells up into a sore, itchy, white lump, which usually disappears after a few days.

DEADLY DEGREE

Mostly just annoying, but can be much more serious.

People sometimes have an allergic reaction, which can be fatal.

WHAT A PAIN!

Fire ants cause all kinds of other problems, too. They dig up parks and yards, destroy plants, and sometimes attack farm animals. They are also well-known for climbing inside electrical equipment and causing short circuits. They can even make traffic signals stop working.

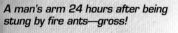
A man's arm 24 hours after being stung by fire ants—gross!

BRAIN-EATING MAGGOTS

Phorid flies are the fire ant's natural enemy. The fly injects its eggs into a fire ant, and when the maggot hatches, it eats the ant's brain! Scientists are experimenting with using phorid flies to keep fire ants under control.

KISSING BUG

Being "kissed" by this killer insect is not very nice. It crawls onto your face in the night, and sucks your blood, usually near your lips. Then, it poops on you before leaving. Yuck!

HORRIBLE HOUSEMATE

Kissing bugs, from South and Central America, feed on other animals' blood. They live in the same home as their host—whether that's a bird's nest, a mouse's burrow, or someone's house. By day, they cluster together in a hiding place. At night, they creep out, looking for their dinner.

A kissing bug enjoys a bloody feast.

KISS OF DEATH

The bite, or "kiss," doesn't hurt, and most people sleep through it. But in the morning, as they rub their face, the bug's dung spreads into the wound, or around their face. Many kissing bugs carry Chagas disease, which has no known cure.

DEADLY DEGRE

☠ ☠ ☠ ☠

20,000 people a year die from kissing bug's affections!

CHILLING CHAGAS

Chagas disease doesn't seem all that bad at first—it's a bit like a mild flu. But the killer germ hides in the heart and other muscles, and can live there for 20 years or more! Eventually, victims can die from heart problems caused by the bug.

BLACK WIDOW SPIDER

The black widow is a spider that strikes fear into humans, with its spooky name and deadly reputation. It has venom 15 times stronger than a rattlesnake's.

FRIGHT IN THE NIGHT

Black widow spiders live in warm parts of the world and come out at night. As well as living in forests, fields, and deserts, they can turn up in homes, yards, sheds, and, sometimes, cars. They don't attack people on purpose—they prefer to hide in a shadowy corner or behind furniture. But the black widow will bite if someone scares it, sits on it, or steps on it.

IS IT REALLY THAT BAD?

When the black widow bites, its small, sharp fangs inject a very deadly venom—but only a tiny amount of it. Most victims feel pain and have bad muscle cramps, but generally survive. Very few bites are fatal—though anyone who thinks they might have been bitten should go to the hospital, just in case.

This female black widow has a bright red mark on her underside.

DEADLY DEGREE

: really as deadly as people think.

WHY "BLACK WIDOW"?

The round, black, shiny female spider is twice as big as the male, and she's the only one with a deadly bite. She sometimes (though not always) eats the male after mating with him—giving her the name "widow," and making her even scarier.

BRAZILIAN WANDERING SPIDER

If you're scared of spiders, look away now! It might not be as big as a huge, hairy tarantula, but this is the world's deadliest and most venomous spider—the Brazilian wandering spider.

WATCH OUT—I'M DEADLY!

This scary spider can grow to around 4–5 inches (10–12 cm) across, and lives in jungles and farmland in South America. When it's about to bite, it puts on a crazy-looking warning display, lifting its first two pairs of legs up high, and swaying from side to side. If it does bite, its venom can occasionally kill in less than an hour—although most people survive being bitten.

BANANA BOX SURPRISE

This spider is also known as the banana spider, because it often hides in banana trees. Sometimes, a spider gets picked along with a bunch of bananas, packed up in a box, and shipped off around the world. It could turn up in a grocery store near you.

DEADLY DEGREE

The deadliest spider of all.

A wandering spider lies in wait on a leaf in the Amazon rain forest.

NO WEB—I LIKE TO WANDER!

The "wandering spider" gets its name because it doesn't spin a web or have a fixed home. Instead, it wanders around the forest floor, searching for prey such as grasshoppers or small lizards.

FUNNEL-WEB SPIDER

In Sydney, Australia, everyone looks out for funnel-web spiders. They often hide in shoes, under piles of clothes, or in watering cans. If they're disturbed, they can give you a deadly bite.

SPIDER FANGS

Funnel-web spiders can be hair-raisingly large—up to 3 inches (7.5 cm) long, with a leg span of 5 inches (12 cm)—and have very big fangs. They can bite through a soft shoe, or even a fingernail. The bite is said to feel like having a nail stuck into you. The venom makes you sweat, shake, and ache, and in severe cases you can't swallow or breathe—which can be fatal.

A female funnel-web attacks a lizard for lunch.

GOING FOR A SWIM!

Funnel-webs are attracted to water. They can survive for 24 hours by breathing bubbles of air that they trap next to their bodies. People fish them out thinking they are dead, and get a nasty shock.

DEADLY DEGREE

☠ ☠ ☠ ☠
✕ ✕ ✕ ✕

Stay clear of the funnel-web's fangs.

FATAL FUNNEL FANGS

Stepping on a funnel-web isn't as bad as it might sound. The spider's fangs point down and it can't bite upward.

DISASTERS, POISONS, AND DEADLY DISEASES

It's not just wild creatures that can be deadly. Our planet is full of terrible toxins; deadly diseases; unpredictable, killer weather; fatal foods; and terrifying natural disasters that can wipe out thousands at a time. It's a wonder so many of us are still here!

FALSE MOREL

This fungus can kill you, especially if it's eaten raw. To cook it, you have to boil it and throw away the poisoned water. While it's boiling, it gives off a deadly gas. And yet people still eat it!

BRAIN ON A STEM

False morel mushrooms are nicknamed "elephant ears," "redheads," or "brain fungus," as they are reddish, bumpy, and wrinkled. Sometimes, people eat them because they accidentally confuse them with edible morels (see box). But some people, especially in Scandinavian

DEADLY DEGREE

☠☠☠

Definitely lethal . . . but only sometimes!

countries, LOVE false morels. They actually cook them as a delicacy.

REDHEAD ROULETTE

The trouble with false morels is that some people feel fine after eating them, while others fall severely ill. The amount of poison varies from one mushroom to the next. Some people eat false morels for years with no problems, then suddenly get sick from one serving. It's all a mystery! But one thing's for sure—the best plan is to not eat them at all.

A false morel doing an impression of a brain.

THE REAL MOREL

The edible morel is a different type of mushroom that is safe to eat. It has a similar wrinkly surface, but it's narrower, and hollow inside. You can sometimes buy these morels in grocery stores.

DESTROYING ANGEL

As its spooky name suggests, a destroying angel is seriously bad news. It's definitely not something you should eat! But what is it?

DELAYED EFFECT

A destroying angel is a small, white, killer mushroom. Besides being deadly poisonous, it looks similar to other wild mushrooms that are safe to eat. So it often fools unwary mushroom pickers. It's extra-dangerous because people who eat it don't feel ill at first. Then, up to a day later, they suddenly feel sick, chilly, and weak. The poison destroys important body parts, like the liver. It can kill in a few days.

SPOT THE ANGEL

The destroying angel is pure white, with a smooth cap, and grows up to 8 inches (20 cm) tall. It often has a thin, ragged membrane around its stem. If you ever see a mushroom that looks like this, do not touch it! As the picture shows, it's impossible to tell which mushroom is poisonous (it's actually the one on the right).

Can you spot the deadly mushroom?

HUNGRY?

Never pick wild mushrooms unless you're an expert. Don't touch mushrooms or toadstools you find growing outside. However, you could buy a mushroom-growing kit at a nursery, and grow your own to eat.

DEADLY DEGREE

☠ ☠ ☠ ☠ ☠
✖ ✖ ✖ ✖ ✖

The destroying angel is one of the deadliest mushrooms around.

POISON PARSNIP

If you don't like seeing a parsnip on your plate, at least be grateful it's not poisonous! The poison parsnip, also called hemlock water dropwort, is seriously deadly.

PARSNIP PARTS

All parts of the poison parsnip are poisonous, but the roots are the worst. Unfortunately, the roots look and taste a bit like real parsnips, while the leaves look like celery or parsley leaves. Because of this, people sometimes collect and eat the plant accidentally.

SERIOUS SYMPTOMS

Poison parsnip is very, very toxic. It makes you feel dizzy and sick, paralyzes your mouth so you can't talk, and can make you have fits and fall unconscious. It can kill in just a few hours, unless the poisoning is treated quickly in the hospital.

DEADLY DEGREE

A particularly perilous parsnip impersonator.

Not nearly as tasty as edible parsnips, and far more dangerous!

THE SENTENCE OF SOCRATES

In ancient Greece, people were sometimes sentenced to death by being given a deadly hemlock drink. The famous philosopher Socrates suffered this fate.

DEADLY NIGHTSHADE

The fat, juicy, purple berries of deadly nightshade have tempted many people to try a taste. Don't be one of them! Eating just one handful of berries could be fatal.

WHAT HAPPENS?

People who are poisoned by deadly nightshade get a dry mouth, terrible thirst, and blurred vision. They start to stumble and feel sleepy. They often lose their voice, and their hands make strange clutching, writhing movements. Finally, they get confused and have horrible hallucinations, before falling unconscious. It's a truly horrible way to die!

A MILLION USES

Despite the dangers, humans have been using deadly nightshade for thousands of years, for all kinds of purposes, good and bad:

- To reduce sweating.
- As a sleeping aid.
- To confuse prisoners so that they confess to crimes.
- As a murder weapon.

A lethal dose of deadly nightshade would make everything look blurry, just like this!

They look like blueberries but you wouldn't want these in a muffin!

DEADLY DEGREE

☠ ☠ ☠ ☠ ☠

A sinister berry surprise.

EYES WIDE OPEN

Long ago, women used to put drops of deadly nightshade potion in their eyes. It made their pupils dilate (get bigger), which was thought to look attractive. Today, it is used to keep the pupil open during eye operations.

CASTOR BEAN PLANT

You might have seen beautiful beans like these strung onto necklaces. They are castor beans, or seeds, and they contain ricin, the deadliest natural poison on Earth.

HOW DEADLY?

Less than a grain of ricin—that's only one milligram—can kill a human. It can kill if you eat it, or inhale it, or if it's injected into the body. It causes pain, vomiting, fits, sweating, and fainting, and most victims die in a few days. Ricin is found in the hard covering of castor beans.

IN A GARDEN NEAR YOU

There's probably a killer castor bean plant growing somewhere near you, right now. Gardeners love them for their beautiful leaves and fruits. People do sometimes eat the "beans" and get poisoned, but it's actually quite rare. The seeds taste horrible, and have to be well-chewed to release ricin.

Pretty, but deadly!

EDIBLE OIL

Strangely, though castor beans contain the deadliest poison ever, they are also pressed to make castor oil, which is edible, and used to make yummy chocolate. The poison stays behind in the shells of the seeds. Castor oil is used to make other useful things, too, like soap, plastic, insect repellent, medicines, and crayons.

DEADLY DEGREE

The most poisonous of all plants, though not the biggest killer.

STRYCHNINE TREE

In movies, poisoning is a sudden, horrific death. The victim's eyes bulge and they foam at the mouth, then fall on the floor, writhing and twitching. Finally, after a last gasp for breath, they perish. But is it the same in real life?

CAN IT REALLY HAPPEN?

In real life, few poisons have such a sudden, dramatic effect—but strychnine does. This deadly poison works by making your muscles go berserk. They twitch, tremble, and tense up at the slightest touch, and it's horribly painful. Victims die with an agonized grimace, from the muscles in their face tightening—scary!

MURDER WEAPON

Strychnine comes from the seeds of the strychnine tree. People have used them for thousands of years, as both a poison and a tonic—a

DEADLY DEGREE

☠☠☠
✕✕✕✕

A nasty murder weapon, but so victims survive.

medicine that perks you up when you're tired. In 1818, scientists found a way to extract the pure strychnine poison from the seeds. It was sold for killing rats.

Don't pick the seeds from a strychnine tree under any circumstances!

FOXGLOVE

You're probably no stranger to this unusual-looking plant—it grows in a lot of yards. But did you know how deadly it can be?

DEAD MAN'S BELLS

You can tell a foxglove by its tall spike of bell-shaped flowers, sometimes called dead man's bells. The plant's scientific name, *Digitalis*, means "fingerlike," as the bells just fit a human fingertip. But DON'T put your finger inside! Besides being poisonous, they are a favorite flower of bees, and there might be one hiding in there. Ouch!

SIGNS OF POISONING

Every part of a foxglove plant is toxic. People have been poisoned after accidentally eating the leaves, or making them into tea. The poison plays havoc with your heartbeat. Another telltale sign of poisoning is that it can make you see weird, glowing outlines around objects.

DEADLY DEGREE

☠ ☠ ☠

Pretty poisonous, so do not touch!

Will this honeybee survive a trip to the foxglove plant?

DR. WITHERING'S DISCOVERY

In 1775, Dr. William Withering heard of a homemade remedy for dropsy, a heart disease. He found that foxglove was the ingredient that made it work. He developed foxgloves into a modern heart medicine, which is still used today. But the dose has to be **EXACTLY** right—too much and it's a killer.

WOLFSBANE

This plant is so deadly, just touching its leaves or roots can make you feel ill. And if you eat it, its powerful poison paralyzes your heart and breathing muscles.

WEREWOLVES BEWARE

Wolfsbane has killed many people who've eaten it by accident—or been poisoned on purpose! It poisons animals, too, explaining the name wolfsbane—or dogbane, mousebane, or even tiger's bane. (If you're wondering what a "bane" is, it's an old word that means a dangerous or deadly thing.) People also thought that if it killed wolves, it must be good for keeping werewolves away! These mythical monsters were said to fear wolfsbane and hate its smell.

DEADLY DEGREE

☠ ☠ ☠ ☠ ☠
✗ ✗ ✗ ✗ ✗

Famous for its extremely lethal poison.

A sure sign of this poisonous plant is the purple "hood" growing on top of the flower.

KILLER CURE

Like many poisons, wolfsbane's killer ingredient, aconite, has also been used as a medicine. A tiny dose could slow down a racing heart. It was also rubbed on the skin to numb pain or itching. This was pretty risky! It could kill if you took too much, or if it got into a cut or scratch and entered your bloodstream.

WARRIOR WEAPONS

In ancient times, warriors dipped arrows and spear tips in wolfsbane juice to make them poison-tipped and extra-deadly. Just a small wound from a wolfsbane weapon could be fatal!

FOOD POISONING

Most people have had food poisoning. Usually, it happens after you eat something that's not cooked properly, or that has gone bad. The food contains germs or chemicals that make you vomit.

IS THAT ALL?

Food poisoning isn't usually serious. But there are some bugs carried in food that can kill people—especially people who are very young, old, or unwell.

- Salmonella, found in raw poultry and eggs, kills thousands a year.

- Toxoplasmosis comes from raw or undercooked meat.
- Listeria can be in cheese, cold meats, and pâté. It can cause dangerous infections.
- E. coli is a common germ with deadly varieties.

KILLER OUTBREAKS

If food poisoning comes from a particular restaurant, or a kitchen in a hospital, school, or workplace, it can cause an "outbreak," affecting a lot of people. By finding out where the victims have eaten, experts can trace the bug back to where it came from, and hopefully get rid of it.

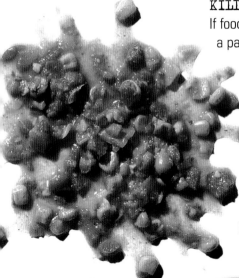

Uuurrgggh . . . food poisoning usually makes you sick.

DEADLY DEGREE

☠ ☠ ☠

...anges from a mild stomachache to crippling, killer cramps.

DON'T GET POISONED!

To avoid getting sick . . .
- **Wash your hands before you cook or eat.**
- **Always cook food properly, according to the recipe.**
- **Keep meat, dairy, and fresh foods chilled—never lukewarm.**

BOTULISM

Botulism is an illness caused by an extremely deadly poison. The poison is called botulinum, and it's one of the most powerful natural toxins ever discovered.

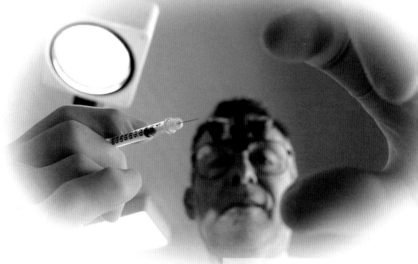

FEELING DROOPY

Botulism is rare, but you can catch it if contaminated soil gets into a wound, or you eat food with the bacterium in it. Once the bacterium is in your body, it multiplies and releases its poison. The first signs of the disease are blurred vision, droopy eyelids, and slurred speech. The poison slowly works its way down the body from top to bottom, paralyzing you.

Doctors inject botulinum in Botox—better hope the dosage is right!

NOT TO PANIC!

You're unlikely to miss these symptoms. Most sufferers are treated in the hospital with modern medicines, so not many people die. There are fewer than 1,000 cases each year. In fact, this poison is used in plastic surgery, in a particular treatment called Botox, where people have it injected under their skin!

NO HONEY FOR BABIES

Scientists have found that there can be a tiny amount of botulism bacteria in honey. It's harmless to most people, but it can affect babies.

DEADLY DEGREE

☠ ☠ ☠ ☠ ☠

One of the deadliest poisons of a

RADIATION POISONING

Radiation can be very useful—we use it in nuclear power stations and hospitals. But it can also be a deadly, silent killer.

WHAT IS RADIATION?

Radiation is a type of energy. It comes from radioactive substances, such as uranium, plutonium, or polonium. It can be a flow of tiny particles, or an invisible energy wave. Very small amounts are OK, but a lot of radiation can make you horribly ill. Radioactive substances can be deadly poisons if they are swallowed. Radiation can also come from atom bombs or damaged nuclear power stations.

WHAT DOES IT DO?

Radiation energy can travel right through your body. As it does so, it knocks pieces off the atoms that you are made of. This damages them and creates new chemicals

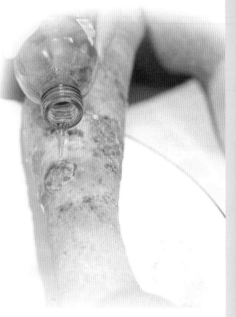

A nurse treats radiation burns still there three years after exposure.

that can cause diseases. A very high dose can kill by destroying the body's organs or damaging blood cells. Lower doses can make cells grow in the wrong way, causing other diseases like cancer.

CHANCES OF SURVIVAL

There isn't a treatment for radiation sickness yet. But, if you survive for six weeks after exposure, you are likely to recover. The bad news is other illnesses caused by radiation don't show themselves until ten years after the disaster.

DEADLY DEGREE

☠ ☠ ☠ ☠

It's lethal, invisible, and hard to control.

RABIES

Rabies is really, really deadly. So deadly, hardly anyone has ever had it and lived to tell the tale. It's one of the most fatal illnesses on the planet.

DEADLY BITE

Rabies comes from animals such as dogs, bats, foxes, and monkeys. If an animal is "rabid" (has rabies) and bites a human, the deadly virus can spread to their body. It takes a few weeks, or months, for rabies symptoms to appear, and there is a medicine that can stop it—but only if it's taken soon after the bite.

STRANGE SYMPTOMS

The signs that a person has rabies are scary. Sufferers drool, their eyes water, and they feel incredibly thirsty—but if someone brings them a drink, they are terrified of it! They start seeing impossible things, and switching between deep misery and mania, or excitement. After this, they usually live only for a few days.

DEADLY DEGREE

☠ ☠ ☠ ☠ ☠

The most fearsome disease caused by a virus.

An untreated rabies bite is usually fatal.

GOING CRAZY

The word *rabies* means "crazy" in Latin. But why does it have this effect? The germ makes animals want to bite—a cunning way to ensure the virus is passed on before the carrier dies.

I'M A SURVIVOR

In 2004, a month after a bat bit her, 15-year-old Jeanna Giese came down with rabies. Her doctors tried out a new treatment, keeping Jeanna in a coma so her body could fight the virus. Miraculously, it worked!

TETANUS

Before it could be treated, this horrible disease usually meant an agonizing death. All the muscles in the body go stiff, and eventually the victim can't rest, speak, eat, swallow, or even breathe.

GERMS IN THE SOIL

Tetanus is caused by a bacterium that's found all around us. It can live in soil, dust, animal dung, or on dirty objects. You can catch tetanus if you get a cut or a deep scratch, and the germ gets in. Inside your body, it releases a killer chemical that makes the muscles tense up.

RUSTY KILLER

People often think rusty objects, such as nails, give you tetanus. But rust doesn't give you the disease. On the other hand, a rough, rusty surface could give germs a good place to hide.

FIGHTING GERMS

Have you ever had a deep splinter? If so, you might have been given a tetanus "booster." This is a vaccination—an injection that teaches the body to fight the germs off, so you don't get the disease. The vaccination has to be repeated every few years. In poorer countries, many people don't have vaccinations because they cost too much. So tetanus is still a big killer.

This super close-up shows tetanus entering your blood through a cut.

DEADLY DEGREE

☠ ☠ ☠
✕ ✕ ✕

Still a seriously deadly disease in many countries.

JAPANESE ENCEPHALITIS

This scary virus can just make you feel as if you have a cold. But if you're very unlucky, it can give you deadly encephalitis, meaning "sore brain."

PIGS, BIRDS, AND RAIN

Want to avoid it? Then don't visit a pig farm in Asia in the rain! The germ isn't just found in Japan, but in India, China, and many other parts of Asia. It comes from pigs and birds, and is spread to humans by mosquitoes. The biggest risk is when it's rainy, because mosquitoes lay their eggs in water. When there are plenty of puddles, millions more mosquitoes breed and bite.

Better to brave a vaccination than catch this deadly disease.

DEADLY DEGREE

Deadly . . . but you have a good chance of getting off lightly.

BRAIN-BOGGLING BUG

Japanese encephalitis is pretty bad news for anyone who has the full-blown version. First, they get a headache, fever, and tiredness. Then, as the brain swells up, they feel dizzy and confused, and might even have hallucinations—seeing things that aren't there. Up to a third of these cases are deadly.

CHILL OUT

There's no cure for this disease. Doctors just have to help patients to rest and keep cool, while they wait to see if they survive. Only 1 in 200 people get the deadly version, though.

EBOLA

Ebola isn't a major killer—so far—but it's a very, very deadly disease. There's no cure, and if you catch it, the chances of it being fatal are between 50 and 90 percent.

WHAT IS IT?

The Ebola virus is a type of tiny germ. There are several forms, and some can give you the illness Ebola hemorrhagic fever. Its horrible effects include pain, vomiting, a rash, and bleeding from the nose, eyes, and ears.

A NEW DISEASE

The first outbreak of Ebola was in 1976 in the Ebola River valley

DEADLY DEGREE

☠×☠×☠×☠×☠

One of the most horrible diseases a human can catch.

in Congo, Africa. The disease is found in some wild animals— humans have caught it from monkeys. But there have been only around 2,000 deaths so far.

Special protective clothing is needed to care for an Ebola patient.

APE TROUBLE

Ebola is bad news for endangered wild gorillas and chimpanzees. It is thought to have killed thousands of them. Scientists are now working on vaccinations.

SMALLPOX

If you lived a few hundred years ago, about one in ten of your classmates would not be around. They would have already died of a terrible, deadly disease called smallpox.

GOOD-BYE, SMALLPOX!

Smallpox gave you spots or "pox" all over and caused fever and exhaustion. Over time, people developed ways of vaccinating against smallpox. They infected children with a mild version of it, so their bodies learned to fight it, and they would not catch the deadly version. In the twentieth century, a huge campaign began to vaccinate as many people as possible to try to get rid of the smallpox virus. By 1980, it was gone from the world's population.

SAVING SMALLPOX

However, two samples of smallpox germs were saved. They are stored under high security in the United States and Russia. People are worried that other countries may have saved smallpox germs, too, which could one day be used as a catastrophic chemical weapon. If that happens, we'll need the saved smallpox viruses to help us study the disease and make new medicines.

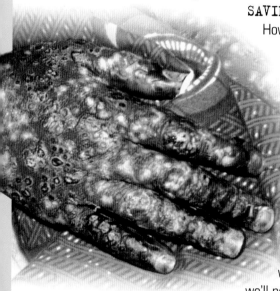

A victim with painful spotty "pox" all over their hand.

DID YOU KNOW?

The most common form of smallpox killed about 30 percent of people who caught it. It's a good thing it has been wiped out and we can't catch it anymore!

DEADLY DEGREE

Once a deadly terror, but now eradicated—well, almost!

BLACK DEATH

Imagine a disease so lethal and infectious, it could sweep through your town in a few weeks, and kill half of the people you know. That's what it was like during outbreaks of the Black Death.

WHAT IS IT?

The Black Death is also called the plague, or bubonic or pneumonic plague. It's caused by bacteria found in rats and other rodents. People catch it when a flea bites them after having bitten an infected rat. Some types of plague can be spread between people, in coughs and sneezes. The disease gives you a fever, aches and pains, and a nasty cough—or strange swellings and black blobs on your body. Without treatment, it can kill quickly, in just a few days.

Horrible buboes, swellings caused by the plague, can appear on legs.

THE PLAGUE TODAY

In the 1300s and 1600s, the Black Death wiped out millions of people, as no one then knew what caused it, or how to treat it. And the plague is still around today. It's just much rarer, as fewer homes are filled with rats, and we have medicines that can cure it.

DEADLY DEGREE

One of the most terrible diseases ever, and still a killer.

EYEWITNESS ACCOUNT

The fourteenth-century writer Giovanni Boccaccio said the plague, "began with swellings . . . They grew to the size of a small apple . . . after this, black or purple spots appeared." He also described how fast it could kill people: "They ate lunch with their friends, and dinner with their ancestors."

CHOLERA

Cholera is essentially the worst stomach bug ever. It gives you such severe vomiting and diarrhea that your body loses vast amounts of water, which can be deadly.

BACTERIA IN THE WATER

You catch cholera by drinking dirty water (or eating dirty food) that contains cholera bacteria. It's a horrible disease to have, but you can actually recover from it quite easily—you just need basic medicine to help your body stay hydrated, and clean water to drink until the disease clears from your body. But, in many parts of the world, people can't get medicine or clean water, so cholera is a death sentence.

Cholera-infected waters in Haiti, following the 2010 earthquake.

WORSE AND WORSE

Cholera outbreaks often happen in refugee camps during wars, or after disasters like earthquakes and tsunamis. In these conditions, there's often no clean running water or working toilets. If cholera starts to spread, the germs get everywhere, as it's very hard to clean up properly, and the outbreak gets worse and worse.

SNOW'S DISCOVERY

In the 1850s, people thought that cholera was caused by unhealthy city air. But a London doctor, John Snow, proved that it came from drinking water. He showed how cholera cases spread out around one water pump in Broad Street, London.

DEADLY DEGREE

A horrific disease when it strikes in the wrong place.

LEPROSY

Even today, the words *leprosy* and *leper* (a leprosy sufferer) sound a bit frightening. For centuries, people were terrified of this disease and avoided anyone who had it. Why?

WHAT IS IT?

Leprosy causes white patches on the skin, damages the nerves, and makes your fingers, toes, and face feel numb. Many people think it makes body parts fall off, which isn't true. But sufferers do often injure their hands and feet, and end up with missing fingers, because they can't feel pain. Some also go blind. Leprosy can kill, but this is rare. Today, it can be completely cured with medicines.

LEPER COLONIES

Long ago, many people thought leprosy was caused by being sinful, or that people who had it were unclean. Sufferers would be thrown out of their families or villages, and had to live in a separate "leper colony" with other lepers. People are terrified of the disease—even though 95 percent of us are immune to it and cannot catch it anyway—phew!

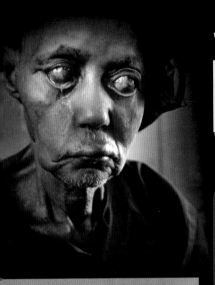

An old man is rendered blind from leprosy—a horrible side effect.

DEADLY DEGREE

Still scares people, yet actually isn't all that deadly.

BLOOD BATH

In the past, people sometimes tried to cure leprosy by drinking or bathing in blood—this didn't work. One of the deadliest effects of the disease was people being murdered to provide the blood for the treatment!

EARTHQUAKE

Earthquakes are among the deadliest events on our planet. In a really big earthquake, nowhere is safe. The ground all around, and everything on it, shakes, breaks, and crumbles.

SH-HH-HH-AKE!
Not all earthquakes are deadly. Some are very mild, and some, even if they are massive, harm no one because they happen in places where no one lives. Earthquakes are most deadly when they strike busy cities. Then they cause buildings and bridges to fall down, killing or trapping thousands of people in their cars, homes, workplaces, or schools. And earthquakes can do even more damage when they cause killer tsunamis (see page 105).

DEADLIEST EVER
The worst quakes in history are:
• Shangxi quake, China, 1556. Over 830,000 were killed.
• Haiti quake, 2010. Over 300,000 people died.
• Tangshan quake, China, 1976. This quake struck while people slept, and killed 250,000.

DEADLY DEGREE

☠☠☠☠☠

One of the deadliest types of natural disaster in human history.

Survivors struggle to cross a bridge following an earthquake.

WHAT IS AN EARTHQUAKE?

Sections of Earth's surface constantly push against one another, and sometimes get stuck. An earthquake is the release of energy when they slip.

SINKHOLE

What if you came home one day to find your house had disappeared—and in its place was a vast, round hole, 100 foot (30 m) deep? Can that really happen?

YES, IT CAN!

Big, cavernous holes, called sinkholes, really can open up in the ground without warning. They've been known to swallow up cars, buses, houses, buildings, and sometimes unlucky humans, too. They have appeared in various places around the world, including China and the United States, where they are quite common.

THE WORK OF WATER

But what causes sinkholes? They form in places with underground rock, like limestone or gravel, that can be dissolved or washed away by water. Water seeps into cracks in the ground, and gradually wears away an underground chamber. If the land above this can't hold itself up, it collapses, opening the hole up to the surface.

DEADLY DEGREE

Very scary, but most are small and don't kill people.

A giant sinkhole caused by rain from a tropical storm in Guatemala.

DOWN THE PLUGHOLE

In 1999, Lake Jackson in Florida drained away down a sinkhole in the lake bed. This has happened several times, but the lake always refills itself!

VOLCANIC ERUPTION

Volcanoes are among the deadliest natural phenomena we face. A volcanic eruption happens when blistering-hot molten rock, or lava, bursts out from inside Earth.

CATASTROPHIC CONSEQUENCE

These are just some of the many ways a deadly volcanic eruption could get you:

- Hot lava—it can be over 1,800 degrees Fahrenheit (1,000 degrees Celsius).
- Flying rocks—volcanoes can fling out rocks as big as buses!
- Pyroclastic flow—a fast, tumbling river of hot gas, ash, and rocks.
- Ashfall—a thick layer of ash that chokes plants, animals, and people.
- Mudflow—volcanic ash mixed with water makes deadly, fast-flowing floods of mud.
- Tsunami—if debris from a volcanic eruption lands in the sea, it can set off a killer wave.

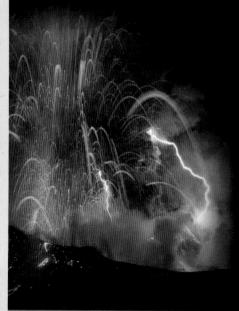

Don't get too close to an eruption: Molten rock spurts high in the air.

DEADLY DEGRE[E]

☠☠☠☠☠
✖✖✖✖✖

Volcanic eruptions have cause[d] many of the worst disasters ev[er]

TAMBORA AND KRAKATAU TERROR

The deadliest eruption in history was at Mount Tambora, Indonesia, in 1815. It killed over 90,000 people—about 10,000 immediately, and the rest from disease and starvation after ash destroyed their homes and farmland. The eruption of Krakatau, Indonesia, in 1883, killed 36,000 people because it caused a tsunami (see page 105).

LANDSLIDE

Can you imagine being buried alive? It must be one of the worst experiences ever. Yet it happens often, when a landslide brings mud, rocks, and soil crashing onto people's homes.

LIQUID LAND

There are several things that can make solid land start to tumble, slide, or flow like a river. After days of heavy rain soaking the soil, or an earthquake or volcanic eruption shaking the ground, large amounts of land sometimes slip downhill. Cutting down trees on hillsides also makes landslides more likely, as tree roots help hold soil in place.

HELP—MY HOUSE!

Landslides can wreak havoc if they happen near towns and villages. The land can slide away from underneath cliff-top houses, leaving them teetering on the edge. Or a landslide can crash down a mountain and land on top of a village. Even if you survive being crushed by soil, you can soon run out of air. Rescuers have to dig people out superfast.

This landslide in Bolivia caused cracks just like an earthquake!

DEADLY DEGREE

☠ ☠ ☠

Some can destroy homes, but most are much smaller.

BURIED TERROR

A deadly landslide disaster struck Vargas, Venezuela, in 1999. Heavy rainfall soaked the steep hills, and torrents of soil and mud swamped several towns. At least 20,000 people died.

AVALANCHE

An avalanche happens when a lot of snow or ice slips down a mountainside. It's an amazing sight—but it's disastrously deadly if it lands on you!

TERRIBLE TRIGGERS

In snowy mountain areas, such as the Alps and the Rocky Mountains, layers of snow build up as fresh snow lands on top of older, harder snow. Sometimes, two layers don't stick together very well. If the top layer gets too heavy—or if a sudden movement triggers it—the snow can give way. Skiers, walkers, and people on snowmobiles set off most avalanches accidentally. The snow can kill people by crushing them, or by burying them so that they can't breathe.

DEADLIEST EVER

The deadliest avalanche in history happened in Peru, South America, in 1970. An earthquake made mighty Mount Huascarán tremble, shaking a huge heap of snow and ice off its top. The giant avalanche landed on the towns of Yungay and Ranrahirca, and is thought to have killed at least 50,000 people.

A terrified snowboarder races to escape an avalanche.

DEADLY DEGREE

☠ ☠ ☠

You can sometimes escape an avalanche, or be dug out alive.

KER-FLUMP!

An avalanche can thunder down the mountainside at 125 mph (200 km/h)—as fast as a high-speed train. It can dump 110,000 tons (100,000 tonnes) of snow at the bottom—on top of you, if you're not careful!

QUICKSAND

People often sink and drown in quicksand . . . in adventure movies and cartoons, that is! Actually, it's really difficult to sink under the surface of quicksand. But that doesn't mean it's not deadly.

WHAT IS IT?

Quicksand is just sand (or grainy mud or soil) mixed with water, from an underground spring, for example. The water pushes the grains apart, so they can't grip one another. If you stand on them, they act like a liquid, and down you go. Shaking makes it worse, so kicking and struggling makes you sink more. However, quicksand doesn't "suck" you down. If you find yourself standing on some quicksand, lie down flat before you sink in—you'll mainly float on top of the sand. You can then wriggle over the surface to safety. If you get stuck, yell or phone for help.

HEEELP . . . I'M STUCK!

It is very hard to actually climb out of quicksand, as it clings tightly around you. This can be seriously deadly. The tide could come in and drown you, or you could get sunstroke, or even become an easy meal for a wild animal. Yikes!

A truck sinks fast—hopefully the driver abandoned the vehicle.

DEADLY DEGREE

Scary, but causes very few deaths, as you can usually escape.

SINKING FAST

It is possible to sink right under quicksand if you're carrying something heavy, like a big backpack—and people have died this way. If you're sinking, throw away anything you're carrying.

DROUGHT

There are few things deadlier than having no water to drink, and no food to eat. And to get these things, we all depend on the weather.

LIFE WITHOUT RAIN

You might not like it much, but rain fills up rivers and reservoirs, and waters the fields. Without it, crops and animals would die, and we'd have nothing to eat or drink. Most places have a regular rain supply or a rainy season. But occasionally, there's no rain for months, or even years, causing a deadly lack of water, called a drought.

RICH OR POOR

Droughts can happen anywhere, but they are deadliest in poor countries. If there's enough money, people hit by drought can have water pumped to them from somewhere else, or can move away. If not, people starve, or have to make long, dangerous journeys.

FATAL FAMINES

The Ethiopian drought of 1984 wiped out harvests and killed up to a million people, though at one point up to 8 million were thought to be at risk of starvation. The Dust Bowl, or the "Dirty Thirties," hit North America in the 1930s. Thousands died from starvation and lung diseases caused by drought and dust storms.

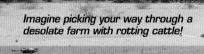

Imagine picking your way through a desolate farm with rotting cattle!

DEADLY DEGREE

☠ ☠ ☠ ☠ ☠

Drought has caused many of history's deadliest disasters.

HEAT WAVE

If you live somewhere chilly, you might think a heat wave would be great! Lots of people love basking in the sun. But did you know a heat wave can be deadly?

BAKING AND BOILING

Heat waves happen in hot summers, when a lot of sunshine heats up the ground and the air, and there's no wind or rain to cool them down.

TOO HOT TO HANDLE

Heat waves can cause heatstroke. Victims feel hot, sick, tired, and dizzy, get a headache or rash, and stop sweating. This can be fatal if they can't cool down. Babies or elderly people are most likely to die from heatstroke.

HOT HORROR

One of the deadliest heat waves on record struck Europe in the summer of 2003, killing 35,000 people.

DEADLY DEGREE

☠☠☠☠

Hot, sunny weather can be surprisingly dangerous!

In a heat wave, even the ground beneath your feet can start to melt!

RED-HOT RISKS

Many parts of the world are pretty hot all the time. People who live in deserts are used to heat—they know to keep cool. A heat wave spells disaster if people aren't used to it.

WILDFIRE

Humans learned to use fire in prehistoric times, and it's transformed our history. It's given us heating, cooking, and rockets. But when it's out of control, fire is terrifyingly deadly.

FIRE IN THE WILD

Wildfires (or bushfires) happen in hot, dry, and windy weather, when trees and plants dry out and warm up until they're ready to burst into flame. A spark from a campfire, lightning, or sometimes a lava flow from a volcano can set them alight. Once it starts, the fire spreads fast. It can burn down homes, or surround people who are trying to escape.

FASTER THAN A SPEEDING BOBCAT!

Wild animals can often run or fly fast enough to escape from bushfires—but not always. When wildfires struck Los Angeles in 2009, they moved so quickly that bears, bobcats, and many birds and small mammals were caught in them, and died.

A firefighter desperately tries to put out a terrible wildfire in California.

DEADLY DEGREE

A horrific killer, but you have a good chance of escaping.

STAY COOL

People prepare their homes for a wildfire by soaking the house and yard with water, and leaving damp towels around the doors. This can prevent the house from burning down.

SANDSTORM

At first glance, the photo on this page looks like a giant wave about to crash over a town. But this isn't water—it's sand.

SAND CLOUD

Sandstorms and dust storms form when a strong wind blows over a sandy desert, or a dry, dusty landscape. It stirs up grains of sand and dust particles into a massive, rolling cloud, up to a mile (almost 2 km) high. As the storm slows, it dumps the sand back down in huge heaps.

GET INSIDE!

You don't want to be stuck outside in a sandstorm. Sand and dust fly into your eyes, ears, nose, and mouth, scratching you and making it hard to see or breathe. It's best to hide in a strong building, with the windows closed. Sandstorms can also crush smaller houses and tents by covering them in sand, or cause deadly car or plane crashes. In Germany, in 2011, ten people died in a car crash when a sudden dust storm struck the highway they were driving on.

This African town will soon be shrouded in dust—run for cover!

DEADLY DEGREE

...ese sand clouds can kill, but hide inside and you should survive.

MISSING ARMY

An army of 50,000 soldiers fighting for King Cambyses II of Persia went missing in the Egyptian desert. According to legend, they were buried by a giant sandstorm.

TORNADO

Tornado winds can pick a person up—or even a horse, a car, or bus—and carry them into the sky. Tornadoes smash buildings to splinters and tear trees out of the ground.

WEIRD WIND

Tropical cyclones (opposite) may be the biggest storms on the planet, but tornadoes beat them for sheer wind power. The wind in a tornado can reach a speedy 300 mph (500 km/h)—fast enough to blast pieces of straw deep into solid wood, or even blow the feathers off a chicken!

TERRIFYING TWISTERS

Tornadoes, also called twisters, have an unmistakable shape—a towering, twisting funnel of wind and dust, reaching from the clouds to the ground. They form out of thunderstorms, when winds from different directions spiral around a thundercloud. Tornadoes can move forward, leaving a trail of destruction, or hop from one spot to another. They're pretty deadly. In the United States, where most tornadoes take place, they kill dozens of people each year, and flatten thousands of homes.

A dark, spiraling tornado sweeps across fields in South Dakota.

DEADLY DEGREE

☠ ☠ ☠ ☠
✗ ✗ ✗ ✗

More intense than a cyclone, but smaller and slightly less damaging.

SKY HIGH

In 2011, a tornado in Alabama sucked eight-year-old Reginald Epps from his bunk bed into the sky, after smashing apart the walls of his house. His family thought they would never see him again—but he landed safely.

TROPICAL CYCLONE

If a gigantic, deadly cyclone is heading your way, you have two choices—run or hide! If you can't get out of the way, you need to find a safe place to hide, fast.

HOT, WET, AND WINDY

Tropical cyclones start over warm oceans, in hot areas near the equator. As the warm seawater evaporates, a lot of wet air rises up. It sucks more air in toward it, creating powerful winds. If the winds get really strong, the tropical storm is classified as a hurricane or typhoon, depending on where it is.

WHIRLING WIND

As satellite pictures show, a cyclone is a giant spiral. The winds whirl around as they are sucked into the storm, and move faster and faster. If a cyclone reaches the shore, it causes havoc. The roaring winds tear down trees and houses, and heavy rain batters the coast. Even worse, a storm surge can flood the land. This is a big rise in sea level, caused by the winds pushing the sea upward.

A tropical cyclone rages over planet Earth.

IN THE EYE

The hole in the middle of a cyclone is called the eye. It's calmer than the rest of the storm. Once the eye has passed by, the wild weather returns.

DEADLY DEGREE

Cyclones have killed millions and millions of people.

ICE STORM

In an ice storm, ice covers every single surface. It doesn't fall from the sky as ice—it falls as ice-cold rain. When it touches the cold ground, it freezes solid, causing all kinds of problems.

ICY DANGERS

Ice storms don't seem as savage as other storms—they can be quiet and peaceful, but they can still kill. Here's how:

• Tree branches snap under the weight of the ice and can fall on top of you—or a whole pile of ice could slide off a building!

• People or their cars slip or skid on icy roads.

• Roads are blocked by ice and fallen trees, which means rescuers can't get through to help anyone who is trapped.

• Power lines break, causing fires or electrocuting people.

• People can get stuck in their houses with no power and freeze to death.

BEWARE OF THE BARBECUE!

Some people have died during ice storms when their electricity has cut out and they have used a barbecue or camping stove indoors to try to cook or warm themselves up. This can fill the air with deadly fumes of the gas carbon monoxide.

Everything gets frozen solid for days during an ice storm.

DEADLY DEGREE

A serious and bitter storm, but the death toll is usually low.

TSUNAMI

A deadly tsunami wave zooming across the land is a scary sight. There's little time to escape as it smashes and flattens everything caught in its path.

A seriously scary tsunami hits the shore in Japan in 2011.

SECRET SOURCE

Tsunamis begin when something disturbs the water in the sea. It could be an undersea earthquake or a volcanic eruption flinging a huge pile of rock into the ocean. This creates giant ripples that spread out in a circle. Each ripple is low, but very wide and fast-moving, carrying a lot energy. When the water reaches the coast, it piles up into a giant wave.

DEADLIEST TO DATE

On December 26, 2004, a terrible tsunami struck in the Indian Ocean. It was caused by an undersea earthquake near Indonesia. The waves hit there first, and spread out to reach Thailand, India, Sri Lanka, and other countries around the ocean hours later. Around 230,000 people were killed, making this the deadliest tsunami on record.

DEADLY DEBRIS

A tsunami carries smashed-up buildings, cars, and boats along with it. Even those who manage to stay afloat in the surging water get battered by the floating debris.

DEADLY DEGREE

A terrifyingly deadly killer.

ICEBERG

"Iceberg, right ahead!" yelled the *Titanic*'s lookout, when he spotted the deadly danger in the dark. But it was too late— the iceberg tore the ship open, and sent it to a watery grave.

ICE MOUNTAIN

An iceberg is a large lump of ice floating in the sea. Icebergs break off from glaciers and ice shelves in cold parts of the world, such as Antarctica and Alaska. Then they float around, slowly melting as they reach warmer seas. *Iceberg* means "ice mountain"—and some are ENORMOUS. One of the biggest ever, named Iceberg B-15, broke off from Antarctica in 2000. It measured 4,250 square miles (11,000 sq km)—that's bigger than some countries!

SPLASH!

When an iceberg breaks away from a glacier into the sea, it can create a huge wave as it crashes into the water. This can capsize small boats.

KERR-RUNCH!

Icebergs are a deadly danger to boats. Most of the iceberg is under the surface, and difficult to see. The ice is rock-hard, and when a boat hits it, the boat comes off worst. The *Titanic* is the most famous example—1,522 people died when it sank in 1912 on its voyage to the United States.

A ship slowly sinks after striking an underwater iceberg.

DEADLY DEGREE

Though huge and lethal, we ca usually sail away from icebergs

RIPTIDE

A riptide isn't actually anything to do with the tide. It's really a rip current—a fast-flowing stream of water within the sea. It's a deadly problem that claims hundreds of lives every year.

HOW IT WORKS

As waves break, they force water up onto the shore, which eventually slips back into the sea. But sometimes, strong winds and waves keep pushing the water up, and it spills sideways until it finds a lower point or channel in the sand. There, it forms a fast-flowing stream, or current, of water, rushing back out to sea. Any beach that has breaking waves can also have riptides.

SWEPT AWAY

Riptides are fast and strong. If you get caught in one, it will drag you out to sea. You can escape by staying calm and swimming sideways, out of the current and back to the beach. Unfortunately, most people don't do this. They panic and try to swim against the current. They soon get exhausted, breathe in water, and go under.

Strong strokes sideways are the best way to get out of a riptide.

SPOT A RIPTIDE

Some riptides look like mini rivers. As a riptide flows out to sea, it can also create a gap in the breaking waves, making the water look strangely calm. Don't go there!

DEADLY DEGREE

A deadly serious danger for unwary swimmers.

LIMNIC ERUPTION

This type of natural disaster is so strange and unusual, you might not even have heard of it. Yet it's devastatingly deadly, in a horrific, silent, and surprising way.

DISASTER AT LAKE NYOS
On August 21, 1986, Nyos village in Cameroon, Africa, was struck by an invisible terror—a cloud of choking gas. It rolled over fields and houses and into nearby villages, too. Over 1,500 people, and thousands of farm animals, were killed.

WHAT WAS IT?
The deadly cloud was made of carbon dioxide gas escaping from Lake Nyos, a volcanic crater lake above the village. The gas had leaked from underground and dissolved in the deep water at the bottom of the lake. Then it suddenly fizzed and bubbled to the surface. This is called a limnic eruption, or lake overturn. Carbon dioxide isn't deadly in small amounts, but animals can't breathe it. It's also heavier than air. So like a flood of water, it flows downhill, suffocating people and animals to death.

Around 3,500 livestock suffocated from millions of tons of gas in 1986.

DEADLY DEGREE

Deadly but rare, so not a great risk to us.

RARE ERUPTIONS
The only other limnic eruption on record killed 37 people at Cameroon's Lake Monoun in 1984. But there are other lakes at risk of eruptions, such as Lake Kivu in eastern Africa, which has carbon dioxide and methane dissolved in it.

WHIRLPOOL

In ancient legends, whirlpools are swirling, gaping funnels that suck ships down to the ocean floor. In real life, they're not quite so deadly. . . .

WHAT IS A WHIRLPOOL?

Most whirlpools are caused by the tide flowing through narrow channels, or over a bumpy seabed. They form only at certain times, when flows of water are rushing past one another in different directions. The water does swirl around violently, but a whirlpool usually isn't big or strong enough to suck a ship underwater. However, whirlpools can spin boats around and even tip them over so they sink!

The earthquake in Japan in 2011 triggered an immense whirlpool over 330 feet (100 m) across.

WHIRLPOOLS OF THE WORLD

These two whirlpool hot spots are the best known on the planet:

• Moskstraumen, a famous Norwegian whirlpool, is said to be the lair of the mythical Kraken sea monster.

• Old Sow, off the east coast of Canada, is famous for its loud, sucking, slurping sound.

DEADLY DEGREE

Fascinating, but less frightening than you'd think.

SOLAR FLARE

Our sun gives us heat, light, and all the energy we need to exist. But it can't always be trusted! A giant solar flare bursting from its surface could trigger a disaster.

ENERGY BURST

The sun gives out energy all the time, but in a solar flare, there is much more than normal. It's a huge burst, or eruption, of high-energy particles, which shoot out of the sun and into space. It's so strong that, if it hits an astronaut in space, he or she could get a deadly dose of radiation and die soon afterward. Solar flares can also damage space equipment, such as radios and satellites.

THE BIG ONE

Most solar flares don't affect us, but a huge one would be different. The high-energy rays could make electrical equipment go into meltdown for months. That would be annoying—we're not used to managing without our TVs or cell phones. But worse, it could be deadly if it damaged hospital life-support machines or air traffic control systems.

Dangerous gases are released from the sun into the atmosphere.

CARRINGTON FLARE

A giant solar flare has struck before, in 1859—known as the Carrington flare. Electrical equipment had not been around for long, but telegraph systems for sending messages were badly damaged.

DEADLY DEGREE

Could be catastrophic, but let's hope we don't face a big one.

IMPACT EVENT

An "impact event" is when a space object—an asteroid, meteorite, or comet—hits our planet. It may sound like science fiction, but it actually happens all the time.

MINI-IMPACTS

Millions of rocky objects zoom around the solar system, and some get pulled in by Earth's gravity. Most vaporize in our atmosphere, but a few reach the ground. Objects less than 33 feet (10 m) across are called meteors, or meteorites if they land on Earth. Hundreds hit Earth each year. Most land in the sea, as it covers about three quarters of the planet. The chance of a meteorite hitting a person is tiny, but it can happen.

MEGA-IMPACT

An object bigger than 33 feet (10 m) across is called an asteroid—and a big one could be seriously bad news. It could explode in midair like a giant bomb, destroying a wide area. It could crash into the ground, gouging out a massive crater and darkening the sky with dust for years. If it was big enough, it could even wipe out life on our planet completely!

TSUNAMI TERROR

A massive asteroid crashing into the ocean would cause the biggest tsunami (see page 105) ever.

An illustration of a mighty asteroid striking Earth's surface—imagine that happening for real!

DEADLY DEGREE

6 out of 5! A worst-case-scenario asteroid would be very deadly.

ACKNOWLEDGMENTS

Marshall Editions would like to thank the following for their kind permission to reproduce their images.

Key: t = top b = bottom c = center r = right l = left bgr = background

Cover: tl, NPL/Nature Production; tr, Biosphoto/Thierry Montford; bl, Alamy/redbrickstock; br, iStock/Jodi Jacobson

Pages: 1 Getty/Paul Nicklen; 2–3 Press Association Images; 4–5 Nature Photo Library/Steven Kazlowski; 6–7 Shutterstock; 7t Getty/Stavros Markopoulos; 8 Shutterstock; 9 Shutterstock; 10 Photolibrary/Michael and Christine Denis-Huot; 11 NPL/Mark Bowler; 12 Press Association Images; 13 Alamy/Chuck Pefley; 14 Press Association Images; 15 NPL/Tony Heald; 16 Getty/James Martin; 17 FLPA/Konrad Wothe; 18 Alamy/John Cancalosi; 19 Shutterstock; 20 Alamy/Mark Newman; 21 NPL/Cairns/Wild wonders of Europe; 22 Alamy/Steve Bloom Images; 23 Corbis/National Geographic Society/Paul Nicklen; 24 Alamy/Kevin Schafer; 24b Alamy/Arco Images GmbH; 25 NHPA/ Daniel Heuclin; 26 Getty/AFP; 27 Reuters/Shamil Zhumatov; 28 Ardea/Ferrero-Labat; 29 FLPA/Sunset; 30 NPL/Edwin Glesbers; 31 FLPA/Minden/Fn/Martin Woike; 32 Ardea/Thomas Marent; 33 Photolibrary/Thierry Montford; 34 NHPA/Ken Griffiths; 35 Photolibrary/Daniel Heuclin; 36 NPL/Miles Barton; 37 Ardea/Karl Terblanche; 38 NPL/Michael D. Kern; 39 Alamy/©SuperStock; 40 NHPA/Ken Griffiths; 41 NPL/Steven David Miller; 42 Alamy/Poelzer Wolfgang; 43 FLPA/Minden/Norbert Wu; 44 NPL/Doug Perrine; 45 Getty/Julian Cohen; 46 Alamy/Michael Patrick O'Neill; 47 Ardea/Ken Lucas; 48 Corbis/Jeffrey Rotman; 49 iStock/Jodi Jacobson; 50 Alamy/Anestis Rekkas; 50b Corbis/©Ocean; 51 Shutterstock; 52 Shutterstock; 53 Ardea/B. + P. Boyle; 54 Shutterstock; 54b Getty/Paul Sutherland; 55 SPL/Georgette Douwma; 56 Corbis/Jeffrey L. Rotman; 57 SPL/A. Crump, TDR, Who; 57b SPL/James Robinson; 58 Getty/Tim Flach; 59 NPL/Kim Taylor; 60 Corbis/Reuters/Pierre Holtz; 61 NPL/ Nature Production; 61t SPL/Scott Camazine; 62 Press Association Images; 63 iStock/Himagine; 64 Getty/Imagemore Co, Ltd.; 65 FLPA/Imagebroker/Olivier Digoit; 66 FLPA/Minden/Mark Moffett; 67 SPL/Scott Camazine; 67c Shutterstock; 68 SPL/Sinclair Stammers; 69 Photolibrary/Raymond Mendez; 70 SPL/Sinclair Stammers; 71 NHPA/David Maitland; 72 Shutterstock; 73 NHPA/Laurie Campbell; 74l Shutterstock; 74r Shutterstock; 75 Alamy/FLPA; 76 SPL/Karen Brett; 76b Ardea/Johan de Meester; 77 SPL/Scott Camazine; 78l FLPA/Parameswaran Pillai Karanunakaran; 78r SPL/Gregory Dimijian; 79 iStock/AtWaG; 79l Shutterstock; 80 Photolibrary/Chris Burrows; 81 Photolibrary/Nick Koudis; 82 Rex Features/James D. Morgan; 83 Corbis/Sygma/Igor Kostin; 84 iStock/Sampsyseeds; 85 SPL/3d4medical.com; 86 Shutterstock; 87 Rex Features/John Le Fevre; 88 Corbis/Phil/CDC; 89 CDC; 90 Alamy/Julio Etchart; 91 Corbis/Yannick Tylle; 92 Reuters/Goran Tomasevic; 93 Reuters/Daniel Leclair; 94 Alamy/redbrickstock.com; 95 Reuters/David Mercado; 96 Photolibrary/Ingram Publishing; 97 Ardea/Pat Morris; 98 Getty/AFP; 99 Rex Features/Lewis Whyld; 100 Rex/Sipa Press; 101 Alamy/©Robert Harding Picture Library Ltd; 102 SPL/Reed Timmer and Jim Bishop; 103 Corbis; 104 Press Association Images; 105 Reuters/Kyodo; 106 Reuters/Handout; 107 Shutterstock; 108 Getty/Gamma-Rapho; 109 Reuters/Kyodo; 110 SPL/European Space Agency; 111 Corbis/Mike Agliolo